WILD LIFE MANAGEMENT WITHOUT TEARS

II EDITION

TRUE STORY OF MOWGLI AND AREA OF THE JUNGLE BOOK

RAM GOPAL SONI

Notion Press

Old No. 38, New No. 6
McNichols Road, Chetpet
Chennai - 600 031

First Published by Notion Press 2019
Copyright © Ram Gopal Soni 2019
All Rights Reserved.

ISBN
Color Edition: 978-1-64678-979-5
Black and White Edition: 978-1-63714-629-3

CONTENTS

PREFACE

I wanted to write this book that is "Wild life Management without Tears", because I felt that innovative ideas in managing wild life areas is very vital for success of the project.

Many a time we don't know what are the factors responsible for decline in tiger and other wild animals from the area and what exactly we should do to help this.

Tourism is one field which I felt is important for the conservation and reducing the man animal conflict by providing employment to all level of local people right from tea shop owner to big Hoteliers and resort owners and lot of youth get employment as guide etc.

This also helps to inculcate the values of wild life conservation and its importance in the society, country and in the world. It also helps to form a positive idea towards conservation in political circle, Bureaucracy and people who matters in state policy and administration. But tourism was seen as against conservation to some extent so I thought to highlight this in my book as it helps conservation.

Pench Tiger Reserve was a sanctuary since 1977 and National Park since 1983, a tiger reserve since 1992 but it was neglected by State because tourists were very low approx. 1000 in the year 2000 as compared to Kanha and Bandhavgarh where tourists were around 50000.

So nobody cared for Pench because it was not popular so very low budget was given and you don't have accommodation for tourists to stay, there were no private resorts except one old Forest Rest House and 4–5 cottages of poor quality.

Unless destination is not popular nobody will invest in private resorts and State Govt. was giving low priority because it was not popular.

As Field Director how I searched an USP (Unique Selling Point) to promote tourism and bring it to not only in lime light but to place this park as number one tiger reserve in India.

I thought to write all those steps and hard work I put to make Pench tiger reserve best wild tourist destination in the country.

Our USP the Mowgli and the area of the Jungle Book, its discovery and true story of Mowgli and the friction novel The Jungle Book written on that background is a matter of great enthusiasm that world should know because The Jungle Book is Famous worldwide people don't know that Mowgli was a real boy existed in the area of Pench Tiger Reserve which was named by Rudyard Kipling a character living with wolves. Sherkhan the villain was a tiger actually existed and which was operating in old road from Rukhad to Kurai and near to Seoni who killed approximately 150 people and was very cunning could not be killed by any hunter at that time which was mentioned in a semi autobiographical novel " Seonee Camp Life in Satpuda Hills" by R.A. Strandel which was named as Sherkhan by Rudyard Kipling.

Rudyard Kipling wrote the Jungle Book in 1897 and he was awarded Nobel Prize of Literature in 1907 for his contribution in Literature and he was the first British to get Noble Prize of Literature and sixth person to get this award of Literature.

I thought to write this book so that world should know the area of the jungle book and true story of Mowgli.

Man, animal conflict is another area which requires special attention to tackle and come up with win – win situation, I tried to highlight certain examples and answer to the problems in this book.

Poaching cases have been on the rise and illegal trade on wild life has become more crucial than even to trade on narcotics. I tried to analyzed this situation and suggested various steps to control by affective informers network.

I tried to highlight various habitat components which are necessary for conservation of wild life. This book will be useful for managers of wild life area, forest areas, students, environmentalists, policy makers and public in general to understand importance of wild life and why it is necessary to conserve nature and wild life for the very existence of Mankind.

– Ram Gopal Soni

ACKNOWLEDGMENT

My gratitude is first to my parents for their love, affection, care and blessings which was solely responsible to make me what I am today. I always admired my revered father late Shri Jageswar Prasad Soni who was my sole inspiration for hard working and a person of correct understanding of Hindu religion who respects all human being and nature. Who was a true follower of Saint Kabir in his understanding of world as a whole?

I remember a story told by him about my Great grand Father Shri Shrikrishna Soni who killed a tiger on foot in the back of a Shitalamai Devi temple 3 km away from my village Birsinghpur District Satna, which must be in a forest at that time. There was a big Tank downside of temple. My Great Grand Father used to go daily in early morning at 5 am to prey the Goddess and take round of temple when he saw a tiger sitting in the back side of temple who opened his mouth and as quick response my great grandfather inserted the whole iron stick in his mouth which he used to carry in his hand and the tiger died immediately. This story went to King which awarded him jamindari of few villages but he was a saint and took nothing from King. May be I was born for conservation of Tiger as my Great Grand Father killed one in defense.

Tiger were so numerous in those days year 1850–60 that it was seen near my village Birsinghpur of Satna District M.P. which is now absent from the district.

My Gratitude to My Satguru Shri Sachidanandji Maharaj Dharkundi district Satna M.P., Whose blessings was always with me and I learnt from him Adhytma and leadership quality and character of Good human being. When I told him that i have appeared in IFS examination conducted by UPSC, he blessed me that you will be selected in IFS, and not only this but before appearing for viva interview I asked him as to how I should be able to face interview board who ask questions in English and I was poor in English communication then he has given advice and blessings by telling that this is a test of officers confidence and not your academic knowledge so if you know the correct answer then reply otherwise tell that I don't know. Due to his blessings I was selected for IFS.

Again when he visited pench Tiger Reserve when I was field director he has written his blessings in visiting book that Pench Tiger Reserve will be ahead of Bandhavgarh and Kanha National Park. His prediction came true and in 2006 Pench Tiger Reserve was evaluated above Bandhavgarh and in 2010 evaluation report of tiger reserves of India it stood first ahead of Kanha National park.

Also I am indebted to The Lord Shiva whom I used to worship when in village. I would like to tell that Lord Shiva came in my Dream when I was preparing for IFS examination at Allahabad in early morning hours around 4 am when I demanded his blessings to make me IFS and he gave his blessing by his hand and words. As per Shastra if you see a dream of God in early morning hours your dream will come true with in short time and I had faith on my God Shiva and I was selected to IFS 1982 batch in Feb 1982.

My sincere gratitude is to my wife shrimati Gyaneshari Soni for her encouragement and taking all pain to carry on house business works along with care of my children with great passion without complaining for my busy service assignments.

Also my gratitude is towards my son Pranay Soni and daughter Pradeepti Soni for their keen advice to write this book and their keen interest for wild life conservation.

My gratitude is towards all my staff posted with me at Pench Tiger reserve Seoni for their valuable support to make Pench tiger reserve a successful wild tourist destination and best tiger reserve in India. My gratitude is to Shri Amar singh Parihar the first Deputy director of Pench National park and my DFO who narrated story of Mowgli and the Jungle book to me when I was probationer in Seoni in the year 1984, which helped me to search USP for Pench in 2001.

I acknowledge my Gratitude to Late Dr. Kailash Narad, History Professor of Rani Durgavati University Jabalpur who told me about Col. William Sleeman and his Pamphlet which he has written in Dharmyug in Jan 1982 edition which ultimately paved the way of Discovery of the area of Jungle book and true story of Mowgli.

I also sincerely thank Mr. Vikram singh Parihar present Field Director of Pench Tiger Reserve for helping me with latest information and Photos of Park.

I also sincerely thank Mr. Akhilesh Mishra Veterinary Doctor and Mr. Bhardwaj of Pench tiger reserve for his contribution of Photos of Wild life of park.

My sincere gratitude to Late Shri Harbans singhji the then Forest Minister of Madhya Pradesh who posted me showing confidence on me to develop Pench Tiger Reserve a known wild tourist destination in India and all my senior officers for their help.

My gratitude is to Mr. Rajesh Patel Junior Engineer from NWDA Bhopal office for helping and encouraging me in writing of this book.

– Ram Gopal Soni

Shri Shri 1008 Shri Param Hansh Swami Sachidanandji Maharaj
Paramhansh Ashram, Dharkundi
District Satna (Madhya Pradesh)

Shri Gavinath (Shiv Ling)
Village Birsinghpur District (M. P.)

Chapter 1

WILD LIFE MANAGEMENT AN OVERVIEW

Wild life management without tears is a book to tell you management of wild life in National park, sanctuary area, tiger reserve and in territorial forests to managers in most simplistic way so as to enable them to do their task with a smile and without tears.

I have not come across wildlife management book which speaks in simple way and help to solve the problems of protected area hence this book.

This is an effort by me on the basis of my experience in wild life field. I was successful as field director of Pench Tiger reserve to take this park in limelight as a new destination for wild life tourism and take this park number one tiger reserve in India in short period of time.

Pench tiger reserve was evaluated as number one Tiger reserve in India in 2010. It was credited for the best water management system and highest prey base population per square kilometer. This book will help to understand the problems and will give you realistic and simple solution.

Wild life management is to manage flora and fauna of the area. But it is beyond that to think what is important for the survival and growth of wild animals in the area. What are the factors which can go against the wild animals?

To make it more clearly wild animals need food, water, space and cover according to their requirement. Manager must have knowledge of pinch period and availability of sufficient water at desired distance.

For example water holes having sufficient water within a radius of 3 km is essential for spotted dear and within 3 to 5 km for Sambhar, Bison etc and that to water must be sufficient for the whole summer season till rains to keep above animals in that habitat.

Animals have knowledge of water resource and accordingly they migrate. Wild pigs need water to drink and mud to cool their bodies by resting and turning round in the mud. it needs natural flowing water to flow and form muddy place below.

Sambhar needs water body for bellowing in December – January during mating season. All herbivores need salt licks in their area for proper health.

Tiger for that matter require lot of Water in the area to stay and hold the area. Bison needs lot of water to drink. Every animal small are big needs sufficient water in their area to last till rainy season.

Many forest managers make mistake in the requirement of water for various animals at desired distance and sufficiency of water availability till summer and by the beginning of rainy season.

They either do not understand or feel that water must be there somewhere. This is very common mistake which forest officer commits. Similarly cover requirement is different for spotted deer than to Sambhar.

Spotted deer need open ground like meadows for their protection in the night but Sambhar can stay in dense jungle.

Similarly breeding tigress needs dense growth, cave, boulder area, with small holes in between boulders to hide their cubs for safety from other carnivores.

[**For tiger to survive in an area it needs sufficient prey base, enough water and dense forest without which it will leave the area and will not survive.**]

Tigers were numerous in central India specially in M.P. almost all the district of M.P. was in habitat by tigers before independence, now tiger is found in dense forest districts of Seoni, Chhindwara, Balaghat, Mandla, Dindori, Shahdol, Umariya, Katni, Jabalpur, Panna, Chatarpur, Hoshangabad, Khandwa, Harda, Bhopal, Raisen, Sehore district but it was wiped out from Gwalior, Malwa and most of Nimad accept Khandwa district and that is due to loss of dense habitat, and prey base. Water is also a great problem.

If we look to the status of tiger from beginning of twentieth century in central India we have records of number of tigers hunted between world war I to world war II for just three princely State Surguja, Korea, Rewa they accounted for hunting of 3000 tigers. Maharaja Surguja Shri Ramanuj saran Singh Dev alone hunted over 1400 tigers and with family and guest accounted hunting 1900 tigers, Maharaja of Korea Shri Ramanuj Pratap Singh Dev hunted 150 to 200 tigers. The last Indian Cheetah, Three young male siblings were shot by Maharaja Korea in 1947. Maharaja Rewa Shri Gulab singhji hunted around 900 tigers. Rewa state is famous for white tiger (Ranjitsingh M.K.2017).

During British period in twentieth Century prior to 1972 when wild life protection act came into force there were hunting blocks which are allotted to various companies or hunters. Alwyn Cooper Company was operating in M.P. In non allotted hunting blocks collector and Assistant collectors can kill tiger by paying 50/- Rupees for tiger and 25/- rupees for leopards.

During 1857–64 Strandel R.A. who has written a book "Seonee, Camp life in Satpuda Hills" wrote that Govt. was paying 20 rupees to hunt a tiger due to large number of man eater tigers presence in the area the cost of good quality rifle at that time was 20 rupees.

Looking to the Onslaught of tigers, situation has reached to such state that we have to save the tiger from extinction though the area has thousands of tigers earlier.

Recent cases of total disappearance of tiger from National park like Panna tiger reserve From M.P. in 2006, Sariska Tiger reserve in 2004–05, Satkosiya tiger reserve in Orissa in 2018, Buxa tiger reserve in 2018 are eye opener as how it happened?

This is total failure of management not to visualize the problem as how to sustain tiger population. Poaching of tiger in these areas were also largely responsible for disappearance of tiger from these areas but low prey base forced tigers to go for outer fringes for cattle kill and was easily poached.

Nauradehi Sanctuary of Sagar district has tigers till nineties but it is not having any tiger now, having an area of more than 900 Sq km. Tiger relocation is on and they introduced one male and a female tigress.

Food, water, space and shelter will be dealt separately in detail as they are the main requirement for survival and growth of wildlife.

Apart from internal factors there are lot of external factors which manager must understand to protect wild animals from poaching and destruction.

Man and animal conflicts are most important factor to be taken into account and are the most important issue to be tackled if we want to ensure protection of wild animals.

Forest fires and deliberate fire by forest staff in the name of early burning need to be stopped if we want habitat productive and useful grasses and leguminous shrubs to remain as good fodder for herbivores.

Human resource i.e. our field staff, temporary workers are to be kept in enlightened, happy, healthy and disciplined for efficient management of wild life area.

Villages inside and outside has to be cooperative and needs to be kept under scanner so that any unlawful activities are not done by them. Compensation of cattle kill by wild predators has to be paid fast to avoid their anger.

Efficient network of informers is very important to prevent poaching of wild animals, they should be from surrounding villages. Grazers who take their cattle to graze in buffer area are the best informer to us, informing cattle kill and presence of tiger etc.

Manager of P.A.s need good relation with territorial wing of forest Deptt. at all levels of hierarchy. Similarly good relation with district administrations is very useful for guarding interest of Protected Area (P.A.). There are many instances when Forest staff was put to problem so this should be taken care of with good managerial skill.

Wild life managers should have full knowledge of his work and about the habits of each wild animal found in his area so that he can understands the management requirement.

It is essential to create awareness among stack holders about importance of wild life especially to political persons in the area; this is a part of awareness program. In democracy public is supreme so we have to take into account the presence of elected leaders of the area to convince them about wild life and its importance.

It will not be out of subject if I tell a real story of my time in Pench tiger reserve Seoni. Inside Pench tiger, lot of fisherman used to catch fish with boats in Totaldoh dam which was a big menaced for tiger. Forest staff use to fight with them to control this but on one occasion dead body of one fisherman was found in dam where staff raided fishermen day before and Fish mafia alleged that their fellow was murdered by forest staff. police registered case against S.D.O., range officer and other staff and started harassing them. My request to police to do fare inquiry has little impact.

Then I narrated this to the then Forest minister happens to be from the same area and I have good reputation with him and told that our staff did nothing so first there should be magistrate enquiry, otherwise Tiger reserve will be doomed due to action against staff when they are not involved.

Minister of forest Late Mr. Harbansh sing was a person who wanted that Pench tiger reserve should become a good tourist destination and I was successful by discovering that area as Mowgliland so he had a very high opinion about me and he helped in ordering Magistrate enquiry by District collector. In due course all the staff was acquitted and we could make Pench tiger reserve as number one in the country, So morale of the story is that excellent relations and good work help to solve the problem and save P.A. area from destruction. This is as well wildlife management because you are not working in isolation but you are surrounded by people and villages.

Public awareness regarding importance of forest and wild life for the society in the form of climate amelioration, rains and water conservation and conservation of biodiversity and gene pool of numerous flora and fauna will help to save wild life.

Wild life manager must have knowledge of all wild animals found in his or her area and their habits and requirements, also understand habitat and its utilization by different animals.

Officer and staff must be trained in present scenario of wild life management and they should be send to different P.A. areas to make them well verse with present day system of management, new technique etc. to deal with their problems when they arise.

Tourism in wild life area now a day's assumes much importance in wild life management. It takes lot of time of managers so it is also a subject matter of wild life management to be taught to new managers. Tourism helps to not only solve the employment of local population which was otherwise dependent on collection of minor forest produce from the area. it also helps in protection as our staff has to be alert because of tourist movement and Deptt. put on extra resources for wild life to be seen in that area. Increase in number of Tigers in tourism Zone was much more as compared to the density of tigers in other areas in Pench Tiger reserve area of M.P.

Knowledge and importance of particular animal help to save them from onslaught of society. Govt. of M.P. permitted to kill Wild boar and blue bull outside forest area with permission in the year 2003 without actually understanding the role of Wild boar for the improvement of habitat.

It happens that honorable chairman and members of public accounts committee visited Pench tiger reserve in 2003 and as field director I was with them during park visit, I told them to see big group of wild boar in the jungle and reminded that state govt. has permitted their hunting without understanding the role of these poor creatures for soil fertility. I told them that wild boars are like plough and puller both in the forest. if you don't plough your farm every year it will become inert, similarly in the absence of wild boar our forest will be inert.

Wild boar use to dig soil and roots for his food and in turn soil working is done which helps in regeneration of seeds. They said that due to ignorance we supported the hunting of wild boar but we will tell that this is not correct. Morale of the story was that if we can explain the importance of wild animals then only we can save them.

> Wildlife management can be defined as the manipulation of wildlife populations and habitat to achieve a goal (Sargent and Carter, 1999). Aldo Leopold defined game management as the art of making land produce sustained annual crops of wild game for recreational use

> "Wildlife" includes any animal, bees, butterflies, crustacean, fish and moths; and aquatic or land vegetation which forms part of any habitat.

NEED FOR STRINGENT PUNISHMENT IN WILD LIFE CRIME

At present punishment for wild life crime is upto three years and minimum one year fine up to 25000/-rupees u/s 51(1). In case of crime against Schedule I or part II schedule II punishment is not less than one year but extend to six years fine 5000 rupees for subsequent offence minimum two years and fine 10000 /- rupees.

Under new amendment in 2006 u/s 51 "(IC) Any person, who commits an offence in relation to the core area of a tiger reserve or where the offence relate to hunting in the tiger reserve or altering the boundaries of the tiger reserve, such offence shall be punishable on first conviction with imprisonment for a term which shall not be less than three years but may extend to seven years, and also with fine which shall not be less than fifty thousand rupees but may extend to two lakh rupees; and in the event of a second or subsequent conviction with imprisonment for a term of not less than seven years and also with fine which shall not be less than five lakh rupees but may extend to fifty lakh rupees.

(ID) Whoever, abets any offence punishable under sub-section (IC) shall, if the act abetted is committed in consequence of the abetment, be punishable with the punishment provided for that offence.".

Looking to the magnitude of wild life crime and fast depletion of wild animals right from prey species to carnivores and our flagship species Tiger and other endangered species, punishment for schedule I wild animals should not be less than 7 years and may extend to life imprisonment, and in case of other wild animals it should not be less than 3 yrs and may extend to 7 yrs and fine up to rupees 2 lakh rupees.

Unless we will not punish heavily to wild life offenders we cannot save our wild animals. Crime against Prey species like spotted dear, Sambhar etc should not be taken lightly and must be punished heavily if we want to protect tiger, Without prey species you cannot save tiger.

Tiger has been wiped out from areas where prey species has been depleted due to hunting. Another reason of prey base decrease is lack of grazing ground and due to invasion of Lantana in forest area you won't find grasses and natural regeneration.

Forest has become degraded and density has been under stocked. Tiger needs three things to survive 1. Dense forest 2. Good prey base 3. Availability of enough Water for all season.

General public should be made aware of importance of wild animals including herbivores so that no body hunts any wild animals and society should act against these offenders and report it to forest department.

All state Government and central govt. should rise to the present need of enhance protection with rapid action force, good vehicles and sufficient budget for protection

MISCONCEPTION ABOUT USE OF WILD ANIMAL ORGANS

Tiger is sought for its bone, blood and Meat. It is a misconception that drinking wine with tiger bone is aphrodisiac and it will enhance sex power in men.

It is due to the wrong interpretation of might of Tiger due to the fact that he mates 40–50 times in a day and this continue for a week, but people don't know that one mating of a tiger lost for 20 seconds only. It is a bad for men and you can say that if mating of men last in 20 seconds then he will be termed as impotent who cannot satisfy his spouse.

So if we tell the people that using tiger bone you're mating will finish in just 20 seconds then nobody will use tiger bone and tiger poaching will be reduced because of its bad effect.

If people in China and other countries want sex power by judging the behavior of wild animal then they should take bone of dogs than a tiger because dog mating lost for few minutes which may be good for men as per assumption of tiger bone to have aphrodisiac property but these are not correct.

People use boil of sloth bear for sex power but it is wrong, it has no such effect. One should instead of using wild animal parts must use herbal medicine prescribed in Ayurveda and they are proven aphrodisiac like Aswagandha (withania somnifera) root powder, Safed Musli (*Chlorophytum borivilianum*) and Sodhit Croanch (*Mucuna prurience*) seed powder. Pangolin or aunt eater smuggling has increased in present for its scale said to have aphrodisiac property which is not correct and it should be saved from extinction.

We have to create awareness among public to save wild life and also govt. should equip wild life and Forest Deptt. with rapid action force and vehicles to prevent poaching.

Charger of Pench: Photo by Mike and Geoff

Badi Mada Tigers of Pench with cubs "Mothers of the Famous Collarwali Tigeress": Photo by Mike and Geoff

Chapter 2

IMPORTANCE OF WILD LIFE

The most important issue on wild life management is the knowledge of flora and fauna of the area, and the role of individual animal in the sustaining of habitat and its use in improving habitat or helping other species of plant or animal for their existence.

This knowledge should be explained to public in most practical manner so that they should realize the importance of species to save them.

If there is ignorance about the role of species then people will not support your cause. Without having knowledge of role of species people do not realize it.

As per Famous ornithologist Dr. Salim Ali, if birds were not there the earth would not have been suitable for human being to live, because the earth will be filled with insects. Birds eat away twice her weight every day and thus keep check on insects. insects eats away and destroy crops and you cannot use insecticide after a limit and even small quantity of use of insecticide goes in food chain causing cancer etc. if General Awareness is created about the role of birds then people will protect them.

WHY WE PROTECT WILDLIFE?

People ask this question as to why they protect wild life. Are they play any important role for survival of man?

And the answer is Yes. Human existence is dependent on the existence of flora and fauna of this planet.

Forest plays direct and indirect role for sustenance of life on earth. Water is the direct fruit of forest. Forest ameliorate the climate and help in rainfall and forest helps to store the water and release slowly in rivers to make them perennial.

Forest is a living store of lot of gene pool of flora and fauna. If there is problem in captive breeding of plant due to pest and insects then it is the wild gene which comes in rescue of captive breed. Rice breed Oraya sativa was almost finished due to pest then gene from wild variety came to rescue of rice.

Bees are responsible for pollination of lot number of species without them these species will be wiped out. Herbivores eat fruits and berries of many plant species and seeds germinate after it is left out in dung's of animals.

Bees are the best example of win–win situation for both plants and bees. Bees help pollination without which pollination cannot be completed and we won't get grains and various fruits.

Elephant is responsible for germination of approximately 30 species of plant in forest area in habitat by elephant.

Wild boars are considered enemy of agriculture fields and a sure cause of concern in man animal conflict. But the role of wild boar is that of plough and plough holder to make the soil fertile for new crop, like in agricultural farm you have to plough the field before sowing the seeds. One plough is required for 2 hectare of land so accordingly we need the number of wild boars needed to plough the soil of entire forest land; otherwise the forest will not regenerate and will get destroyed once the mature trees die. Hence wild boar is very important for the ecosystem. Wild boar from his mouth dig up the roots of trees and soil to get his food and intern soil get ploughed and becomes fertile due to enhance aeration so this is creation of God to help nature by habits of an animal.

Our fore fathers have minutely observed these things and conducted their work in such a way so that without disturbing wild boar they were cultivating a variety of rice known as Kardhi and some other similar variety which is not eaten by Wild boars in such areas near forest and wild life areas. This rice variety has spines in it so not eaten by wild boar but it is very nutritious though it is reddish in color.

Similarly Black Bucks are found in agricultural land. I have seen plenty of them in Seoni District in over an area of 50000 hectare where soil is shallow and from ancient time people were cultivating Horse gram and black bucks use to nibble and this results in increase in number of branches and hence more crop. This was symbiotic relationship between farmers, horse gram crop and Black Buck and question of man animal conflict did not arise but now people started sowing soybean which is destroyed by black buck. So who is at fault?

Birds are very important for us as they keep control of insects who destroy our crop. But people due to ignorance kill birds without understanding the roll of birds as insect eater. Our earth will not be fit to live by human beings as it will be full of insects. This has to be told to society so that they help to protect birds. Without birds how much insecticide you will spray? Insecticide enters our food chain and cause cancer and other ailments.

There are numerous example of importance of wild life and there has to be understanding as to how you can keep a balance between nature and your agriculture. Human race need wild life, its flora and fauna for its very existence.

Bison herd: Photo by R. G. Soni

Tiger: Photo by Pranay Soni

Tigress with Cub: Photo by R. G. Soni

Submergence Area: Photo by R.G. Soni

Dense Forest: Photo by R. G. Soni

Chapter 3

DESIRED COMPONENTS OF WILD LIFE HABITAT

Habitat is the place where an organism or community lives; it is a spatial entity on the surface of earth. A habitat can be visualized as a macro habitat or a microhabitat. Wild life manager has no control over macro habitat but it can reasonably manage micro habitat like landscapes, thickets, trees, grassland etc.

Habitat of wild life includes Food, water, cover and space. In order to survive in an area and for their sustainable development above four things are extremely essential.

Manager must know as to what is the requirement of different wild animals to sustain in that area. We will first take up the issue of food.

FOOD

There is different food chain among wild animals and accordingly requirement of different species is determined. Herbivores, grazers and browsers need different species of plant to feed on. For example spotted deer are predominantly Grazer and it requires large meadows where as Sambar needs dense forest and bushes to brows upon apart from grazing.

Bison are Grazers and browsers both, it prefers bamboo forest and hilly terrain. In summer it needs lot of water and good water body which can last upto summer.

Tiger and other carnivores need sufficient prey as herbivores otherwise they move out of the area in search of cattle and thus are exposed to poaching. Though cattle are important food and contribute more than 20% of their food.

Sometimes we ignore the requirement of Tiger and other carnivores and proportion of population available as kill. One Tiger requires 70 spotted deer unit per year for its healthy sustainability and a leopard needs 40–50 spotted dear units per year. Similarly wild dogs, wolf etc. need quite a good number of prey base.

Not all herbivores are available as hunt and approximately 10% of prey population is available for kill. There are number of species like wild boar, Sambar, Bison, etc. are also available for hunt.

We have to calculate the availability of prey population for a number of carnivores to be sufficient for them.

If we find that there is paucity of herbivores then measure to improve habitat for increase in population so that a proper balance is maintained.

Cattle is considered an important prey base for tiger and panther and it proportion is as high as 20 to 30%. In Gir national park cattle prey for lion is more than 60% because of easy availability of cattle reared by Maldharies in side Gir sanctuary.

Tigress with small cubs goes to buffer area for cattle kill to feed cubs and herself. Tigress with 3 to 4 growing cubs needs more food and they cannot be fully fed by hunting spotted deer and Sambar so it resorts to killing cattle. In Pench tiger reserve a tigress with 4 growing cubs was hunting cattle in buffer area in jamtara – Gumtara area though there are quite good number of spotted deer and Sambar inside Park. Tigress eats only after all cubs are fully satisfied and if nothing is left she can remain hungry, will try to kill another prey.

Once the cubs are more than 6 month old she will let them try to hunt and tigress will assist and train them and during this training in one instance 13 spotted deer were killed in one day by 4 cubs and one tigress in Pench tiger reserve.

Tigress is more fond of killing male Sambar as it gives preferred meet and more to eat. So it is wisely said that if Sambar is their tiger will follow soon.

In order to have tiger in that area you have to create condition favorable to Sambar like it must be dense forest, with water throughout year.

For good population of spotted deer we must have open grassland and water within 3 km radius. Generally we forget this important factor for spotted deer to flourish.

If there are dense forest so we must create open grass land area by cutting tree growth where trees are sparse and grass land should be well distributed in whole area and at least every 5 km area we must have good grassland and water body which retains water round the year.

Panther and wolves are active between forest and villages mostly and they prey on goats, sheep, dogs and other cattle like cow, buffaloes etc. occasionally panther attacks human being specially women and children and in process becomes man-eater

Many tiger reserve lost tiger population because of low or negligible prey base. Due to lack of prey base tiger stray outside core area and to village areas and poached by hunters, electrocuted, poisoned.

So, sufficient prey base population is very important for the survival of tiger and other carnivores. Wild life manager must look into this aspect to sustain tiger population.

Good grassland with palatable grasses, sufficient water bodies, salt licks are essential for increase in prey base population.

In M.P. early burning of grassland in Kanha has resulted in depletion of grass land and due to repeated burning coarse grasses replaced palatable grasses and many leguminous species found in the area vanished resulting in to low prey base population and lesser number of tiger population.

WATER

Water is the most important component of wild life habitat and is critical for presence of wild animal in any area. We usually do not visualize this in totality and could not assess the water requirement of wild animals.

If a river is flowing inside of a protected area that does not mean that it is sufficient for the area wild animal of the area. Spotted deer needs water with in 3 km if they stay there apart from grazing ground and open meadow. Sambar and Neelgai can tolerate water presence upto 5 km.

Assured water till start of rainy season is the first and foremost important requirement for wild animals to remain in the area.

Water is very important for tiger and that to assured water in the area is prerequisite for presence of tiger.

As we know that water is very scarce in forest area specially in summer and in many areas after December you don't see water over ground because of soil being sandy etc. Water goes down in subsoil and is not available for wild animal.

Water can be seen in few places where they can drink water but this leave some area underutilized and other over utilized. Due to overgrazing grasses start deteriorating.

Similarly more than one male tiger can use this area which results in infighting between them.

This is common problem in almost all park and sanctuaries.

Here comes the role of wild life manager to act to provide water for wild animals of the all area in effective way.

How to provide water?

General practice which i have seen in national parks is to make soccer at some places near main road and supply water through tankers.

I have seen this practice in Pench tiger reserve where they had made few dozens of cement soccer and water was supplied through 20 odd water tankers every day. Where diesel vehicles are not allowed diesel tankers were used to supply water in the park.

Disadvantage of this system

Water in cement soccer becomes very hot and it is not drinkable in noon, and water is limited sometimes could not suffice for 24 hrs and for all animals.

Another system used was hand pump and soccer where a daily wager is employed to pump the water and it is filled in soccer 20 to 30 feet away by water channel.

This is better but two things are bad in this, one is that water becomes hot and another is that human presence is always there and people going for safari seeing man did not feel wilderness.

Looking human being inside park pumping water his feeling of wilderness goes, so this is again not a natural way of water management.

What is the best way?

When I joined Pench tiger reserve as field director in the year 2001 park was facing water scarcity. There was only one small tank which retains water upto January. Pench river flows in the middle of the park which bisects forest in Seoni and Chhindwara district and water is available in river and is utilized by animals 3–5 km from the river.

411 sq km area of park does not have water over ground due to sandy soil. So the practice was to supply water by water tanker in soccer.

As an innovative idea I told to dig small waterhole called jhiriya where ever water comes out at least one such jhiriya in 3km radius be constructed in the park and sanctuary.

Jhiria is the best way of making water available to wild animals in distant forest area. Water is very cool and remains for whole summer.

Where we should dig jhiria?

Jhiria should be dugout in a small valley area in the banks of small stream where tree of such species is there, like tree of Arjun (*Terminalia arjuna*), Saja tree (*Terminalia tomentosa*), Jamun tree (*Syzygium cumini*) or in the places where grass is green and bees are sitting there.

If you dug a water hole round in shape 5–6 feet deep 5–6 feet diameter you can find water which will fill up the pit and will flow down.

Water of this will be very cool even in hot summer and water is liked by wild animal, it is inside forest and without disturbance. Once it is dugout, we don't have to go for filling the water but we can just go for patrolling and cleaning occasionally.

Approximately hundreds of such type of jhiria were made in the park all over by staff and we stopped water tanker supply from next year onward.

Mr. Gautam Soni Game guard was given out of turn promotion to become forester from Forest Guard because of his work to make such waterhole in a hilly area where there was no water, and his name was recommended by me for doing exemplary work. This felicitation of one staff spark enthusiasm to all staff and that is how we could dugout 100s of jhirias and we stopped water tanker.

What is Next step for having enough Water?

1. Nala Bandhan (Stream check dam):-

In central peninsular India, water flow in streams stops by the end of October. Because soil is sandy so water goes down in subsoil strata. Small streams flowing inside the park should be dammed by making small dams at 1–2 km interval where ever possible.

These check dams should be made across the Nala (stream) and there soil should be dug out to reach hard strata i.e. 2 to 3 feet deep and black cotton soil should be used to make puddle then dam is constructed giving waste weir to release extra water. This way we have to create series of small dams so that water is stopped inside park. We can dig small jhiriyas down each dam after water in small dam dries up. This ensures water availability round the year inside the park at remotest point and we need not to employ disturbing water tankers for supply of water.

2. Construction of small tanks:

In order to ensure water availability round the year we have to construct such type of small tank at appropriate places so that water is available in 3 km radius and the entire habitat is properly utilized.

Selection is the most important of all things for constructing tanks. Some of the important points are to be kept in mind.

Place where we will dam the water across the stream should be as far as possible narrow and where you can find hard strata within 3–4 feet down the earth, and have good soccer shape area to store enough water.

You have to dig a trench 6 feet wide across the stream going 10 feet deep inside both the bank side. You have to fill this trench by black cotton soil puddle.

Bring black cotton soil and spread it and water is poured so that soil can form lump. Laborer has to walk in it to mix it properly so that you can make cube like earth.

This cube of black cotton soil is filled in trench upto full tank level. After this black cotton soil on both the side is placed and spraying of water is done along with pressing by wood stuff to make the dam hard. Pressing by flat wooden piece of timber has to be done after height is raised by one foot after spraying water in it so that dam becomes compact, It is known as compacting.

Waste weir has to be of proper width and depth so that it can release extra water from the dam. Stone pitching has to be done inside of dam facing water from bottom upto the top to save dam from force of water. Waste weir can be made by concrete so that flowing water does not damage the dam.

This process of constructing tank or small dam was written in the book," Sconee camp life in Satpuda hills" by Strandel the famous writer of "Mamalia of India ". He was narrating a storey of Seoni district. In the year 1864 when a Deewan was passing through Rukhad ask villagers about water and was told that here water goes down inside the earth due to sandy soil of the area.

There is always water crisis so Deewan got permission from then administration to construct a tank by the given process. He has written that due to Pudlling made of black cotton soil upto hard strata down does not allow water to leak out and so you can store water in this tank till summer.

Taking this clue all the 25 odd tanks were constructed on this method, and all are successful. If you find that catchment is less and water will not last till summer then we can have tube well operated by solar pump if there is water in 100–150 feet according to the capacity of pump.

3. Construction of Dyke in area of submergence of a Dam:- Dyke was constructed in the neck of small stream meeting the big river. This was felt necessary because due to submergence wild animals has to walk long distances in open ground and it is more difficult in summer. Moreover there is marshy land in the banks of river in submergence area of a dam. So it is difficult to drink water by wild animal and many a time they are drowned and dye in marshy land.

So it was thought to have dyked so that water is available upto tree line. This is ideal for herbivores as well as good hunting ground for tiger.

We constructed three dykes in Pench Tiger Reserve and are the best place for breeding tigress.

Method of Construction of Dyke as invented by me in Pench Tiger Reserve area

Earlier concrete dyke was proposed to be built at the cost of 40 Lakh rupees under eco-development program in 2000–2001, But when I joined in the year 2001 found this proposal being rejected by world bank authorities, I thought to construct it by local material in an innovative way.

At that time in the month of February – March submergence water was there and depth of water was 15 feet at neck of the Nala, and river was flowing touching top banks at both side.

I advised my staff to bring approximately 1000 empty jute bags used for tendu leaves packaging and we will fill this bag with puddle black cotton soil cubes and then they will be placed in the neck of Nala from bottom to the top in two rows. next layer will be across first one in chessboard pattern so that it is compact. after this layering reached over water level then we will pressed it by rolling a jeep.

Water was stopped perfectly with very little seepage. We did make waste weir from one corner so as to release extra water in rainy season.

This was the successful innovation and water remained for round the year and dyke one at Alikatta was constructed with Rupees 35000/- cost. Another Dyke in Alikatta area was constructed at the cost of rupees 50000/-, both the dykes are life line of Pench tiger reserve.

Dyke can be constructed when submergence is not there and water has receded. At that time you can construct dyke by the same method as of making small tank by having core of the dam by black cotton puddle upto full tank level or by the method of dyke construction given above.

This innovation was replicated in many parks in Maharashtra and M.P.

Water availability in abundance throughout park area at 3–5 km radius is the key for successful wildlife management, because water is most important for life of animal.

If there is scarcity of water then prey species number will reduce and so it will not support enough number of tigers. Water is the limiting factor for wildlife to flourish. If manager could understand this simple thing and apply his mind on above narrated methods he will succeed in successful wildlife management.

Salt licks:-

There are natural salt lick areas in the forest where soil is salty and they are very important for vitality of animals. Salt licks near water hole are boon to the herbivores.

If there are no saltlicks then we can supplement it by putting saltlick bricks from market and it is tied by a rope so that it is kept there.

Regular patrolling is very essential to these waterholes so that nobody can put poison in water body especially if waterhole is small.

COVER

The term cover has been defined in various ways in the context of wild life management. Essentially, it can be considered as a variation seen in a habitat, which affords protection to animals from the weather, predators or enemies by offering a better vantage point (Shaw, 1985). The term "cover" means vegetative or other shelters for wild life.

Cover is for safety of wild animal. some animal need dense cover but many other herbivores need open ground as cover for safety. Sambar need dense forest and hilly area, its organs are so that it can hear the sound due to its big ears. Moreover dense cover relates to its feeding habits. Browser species need dense canopy.

Spotted dear need dense and open both. In day time it feeds inside forest as well as in open grassland. In dry season because of non availability of grasses it is dependent on monkeys who throw leaves and fruits from trees. Both have symbiotic relations as monkey gives alarms of tiger movement but spotted deer give call of leopard who is enemy of monkeys and it can climb trees so deer give clear alarm of panther to monkeys.

Herbivores are dependent on monkeys in dry season to get leaves of trees so trees which are good fodder are important as cover to herbivores.

Cover is important for infants of deer to save them from carnivores. That is why they hide their young ones in high grasses and they graze nearby.

Cover is important to tiger cubs for safety so tigress use to hide their cubs in caves with narrow openings so that cubs are safe when she is away for hunting for whole night. I have seen a tigress coming back to the cave in the morning after hunting for whole night. on her voice cubs came out and tigress with full affection started feeding them.

Tigress gives birth in such an area where there is good hiding ground and drinking water nearby.

Fox, jackal wolf and wild dogs need caves to hide their young ones.

There are different types of covers

1. **Refuse cover**
2. **Ambush cover**
3. **Loafing cover**
4. **Breeding cover**
5. **Roosting cover for birds**

Refuse cover: - Dense Vegetation act as refuse to animal

Ambush cover: - Used by Carnivores to ambush herbivores.

Loafing cover: - Some secluded place of rest in certain point of time in a day. Sambar sits out in high hillock in mid day in a shade of trees.

Breeding cover: - is used for breeding purpose by various animals and is of different type for different animals

Roasting Cover: Roasting cover is mostly used by birds where thousands of birds take rest. It may be ground or it may be trees.

So cover is very important for survival of various species.

SPACE

Animal requires physical space to live. Its day to day requirement like procurement of food, water; cover and mates are met from this space. The amount of space required depends upon the population size, habits and body size of the animal species and the diversity available in the habitat to meet the various requirements.

Space is again an important for requirement of a good habitat for species. Spotted deer can move 3 to 5 km where as Sambar may need 5 to 10 km to move about for food, safety or cover. Tiger and tigress need variable territories depending upon availability of prey base.

Male tiger need at least 8 to 10 square kilometer area as its territory. Two to three tigresses can coexist in side territory of a male tiger. Male tiger wander to as much distance as more than 300km.

Tiger explore new territory and keep on moving his territory as if to defend his kingdom and to save his area from any other intruding tiger. These results in territorial fights between two male tigers sometimes it is fatal. Young male oust older male from his earlier territory so old tigers are pushed to outer area in buffer of park. These old tigers tend to hunt cattle and become cattle eater due to their inability to catch wild animals.

Big space is needed for young and powerful male as compared to old and less powerful male. Area of territory of a tiger depends also upon availability of prey base in that area plush power and strength of a tiger to expand his territory.

Fanning out population of tiger in buffer area needs protection and proper habitat with water and sufficient prey base to hunt. Wild life manager must visit buffer area and make such arrangement so as to have a good habitat with sufficient water and prey base and keep close watch to poachers.

Hand pump: Photo by R. G. Soni

Saucer: Photo by R. G. Soni

Jhiriya: Photo by R. G. Soni

Nala Bandhan: Photo by R. G. Soni

Dyke: Photo by R. G. Soni

Alikatta Tank: Photo by R. G. Soni

Jhiriya: Photo by R. G. Soni

Tank: Photo by R. G. Soni

Toyeair Tank: Photo by R. G. Soni

Dyke: Photo by R. G. Soni

Garari Forest: Photo by R. G. Soni

Dense Forest Cover (Kala Pahad): Photo by R. G. Soni

Bison Herd on the Road: Photo by R. G. Soni

Chapter 4

SOME IMPORTANT WILD ANIMALS OF CENTRAL INDIA AND THEIR HABITS

We would like to give details and habits of some of the wild animals found in Central India to understand them and their requirement for better management of wild life. Managers of P.A. and forest must understand the habits of different wild animals found in the area and their requirement of habitat.

TIGER

Panthera Tigris (Linnaeus)

In Hindi it is called Bagh, Sher. Average Length of Tiger measured in a straight line between pegs is 9 feet 6 inches (275–290 cm) and may exceed 10 feet (300 cm).

Average Weight of male 180–230kg, female 45 kg less (135–185 kg). (Prater S.H., 1980).

The Indian Tiger is rich colored well striped animal found practically throughout India from the Himalayas to come Comorian, except in the deserts of Rajasthan.

Habits: In India the tiger has left its tracks in the winter snows of the Himalaya at an altitude of 10000 feet. It lives in humid evergreen forest, in dry open jungle, and in the grassy swamps of the terai, while in the Sunderbans it leads an almost amphibious life in a terrain of trees, mud and water.

Three things are essential to the tiger, the neighborhood of large animals upon which it can feed ample shade to sleep in and enough water to quench its thirst.

Ordinarily the tiger hunts between sunset and dawn. It hunts game of all kind gaur, buffalo, deer, neelgai, wild pigs, bears and porcupine and will kill and eat panthers and other tigers. Driven by hunger it will eat almost anything, fowl, fish, reptiles, or carrion. In the absence of game animal it can resort to killing cattle. Tigress to feed its cubs mostly kills cattle.

Tiger when become old does resort to cattle kill. It can become man eater if it occasionally killed a human and then resort to killing humans. Normally it does not attack human being unless they stumbled upon him. In order to protect himself from tiger one has to move making sounds.

Tiger is polygamous and 2 to 3 tigresses are mostly found in a male tiger territory. Tiger mark his territory by spraying his urine in tree and also by scraping trees of Sterculia urines(Kullu) or any such tree with soft bark at height so that to show to any intruding tiger about the presence of big tiger and his territory.

During mating they go near water body and it last for a week. Usually one mating time for tiger is just 20–30 seconds i.e. very short but it takes ride over tigress for mating from 40–50 times in a day.

Gestation period of tiger is 105–110 days and 2 to 6 cubs are born. Average is 2–3 but with good prey base and health of tigress it gives 3–5 cubs. In Pench tiger reserve famous tigress gave birth to 5 cubs all survived. Majority of cubs are born between February and May.

Cubs stay with their mother upto 2 years. Sexual maturity of tigress is 3 yrs where as for male tiger is 4 yrs.

Tigress is a strict mother and when cubs are small below 6 month they are kept in a cave with small wholes so that no other carnivore can inter and kill her cubs.

She wanders whole night for hunting and comes in the morning at dawn time and with her slightest noise all cubs comes down to mother to sulk milk.

Male tiger do not kill his cubs but intruding tiger can kill cubs so that tigress can come in heat. Unless tigress leaves her cubs after their age is 2 years it will not do mating with any tiger. One Adult tiger needs between 60–70 spotted deer unit in a year, it has to do hunting after 4 to 5 day. It eats kill for 2 to 3 days depending upon weight of kill. Its favored kill is Sambar and wild pig. We can assume as to how many deer is needed for a number of tigers?

THE LEOPARD OR PANTHER

Panthera pardus (Linnaeus)

It is called tendwa in Hindi, Chita etc the average length is 7 feet(215cm),females about one feet(30 cm) less, an exceptionally large male may reach upto 8 feet(245 cm). Weight 150 pound (68 Kg) female about 110 pounds (50kg) (Prater S.H. 1980).

A typical panther from the Indian peninsula is a sleek short haired animal with a fulvous or bright fulvous coat marked with small close -set black rosettes.

The Indian Panther ranges over the whole country and extends into Burma and Ceylon.

Habits: Panthers are able to live and thrive almost anywhere. They are not restricted to forest or heavy cover like tigers, and thrive as well in open country as among rocks and scrub.

They frequently hunt in day particularly if it failed in night. The panther will kill and eat anything it can overpower with safety, cattle, deer, and monkeys, smaller beast of prey and larger rodents like porcupines. IT also kills birds, reptiles and crabs. The panthers chief enemy is tiger.

Panthers living near human settlements outside forest prey mainly on domestic animals, calves, sheep and goats, on ponies and donkeys and quite commonly on dogs.

Panthers living in forest which preys on wild animals behave similar to tiger. It takes its quarry to a tree to safety. Its power is amazing.

Panther breeds all the year round. Gestation period is 87 to 94 days (prater S.H. 1980) and normally 2 cubs are born but occasionally 3 to 4 cubs may be born.

One panther needs 40–50 spotted deer equivalent prey in a year.

THE WOLF

Canis lupus (linnaeus)

It is called Bheriya, nekra, bighana.

Size: Height 2 feet, 2 inch to 2 feet 6 inches (65–75 cm), body length 3 feet to 3 feet 6 inches (90–105cm) Weight 18–27 kg (Prater S.H.).

Its size, large skull, and teeth distinguishes the wolf from the rest of the family. Animals from India have sandy fawn coats stippled with black.

Distribution: Europe, North America, northern, central and south–western Asia. Within Indian limits, Tibet, Laddak and parts of Kashmir, extends into the desert zone and dry open plains of peninsular India.

Habits: Wolves may live in forest, but in India they are more common in bare and open regions. In the barren uplands of Kashmir, Laddak and Tibet they live as nomads coming down to the valleys in winter, migrating with game and grazing flocks to the snow line in summer. In these parts holes, caves and cavities in rocks provide them with shelter in winter. In the Indian deserts wolves' shelter from the heat in burrows dug in the sand dunes.

Elsewhere they remain above ground, lying up in fields or patches of scrub and thorn forest.

Wolves hunt by day or by night. Wolves prey mainly on cattle, sheep and goats.

The main breeding season is at the end of the rains and majority of cubs are born in December. Three to 9 whelps are born in a litter. The duration of life is 12 to 15 years, wolves are easily tamed.

THE JACKAL
Canis aureus

It is called Gidhad or Shiyar in Hindi Height about 15–17 inches (38–43 cm), Head and body 2 feet-2 feet 6 inches(60–75cm) tail 8–11 inches(20–27 cm):weight 8–11 Kg (Prater S.H. 1980)

The jackals long drawn eerie howling at dusk or just before dawn is a familiar sound in the villages but due to poaching its sound is now becoming less and less. Its coat is typically a mixture of black and white washed with buff about the shoulders, ears and legs.

Habits: It is found throughout India it can live in almost any environment, in humid forest country or in dry open plains or deserts. They have been found at a height of 12000 feet in the Himalayas.

Greater number live in the low lands, about towns and villages and cultivation, sheltering in hole in the ground. Jackals usually comes out at dusk and retire at dawn, but in cool or cloudy weather they may be seen in day time. Sometimes they form packs but usually go about alone, or two or more may hunt together.

They do good work in the clearance of carcasses and offal with vultures.

I have seen jackal chasing a fawn of chital with great speed. They can kill lambs, sickly goats and sheep, become poultry thieves. It eats fallen fruit of ber. Duration of life is 12 years.

INDIAN FOX

Vulpes bengalensis

It is called Lomari in Hindi. Length of Head and body 45–60 cm and tail 25–35 cm weight 1.8 kg to 3.2kg (Prater S.H. 1980)

This is the common fox of the Indian plains, a pretty, slender -limbed animal, smaller and slimmer in build than red fox, distinctive in the black tip to its tail. The backs of its years are generally of the same tone as the head and nape, never jet black.

Its general color is grey, purer grey in winter, contrasting with the rufous limbs. It is found in whole of from the foothills of Himalaya to Cape Comorian.

Habits: The Indian Fox keep to open country and rarely enters forest. It is common in the waste and scrub of our desert Zone, but not in true desert.

It lives in waste land and cultivation, rocky hills and broken country. The Indian Fox lives in a burrow dug by itself in open ground or in scrub.

The burrow always has several openings, some blind, others leading to central chamber, 2–3 feet below the ground. Here fox sleeps by day coming out at dusk to seek its food. In the gathering darkness it's chattering bark is herd, a sharp yelp, repeated three or four times. Its food consists of small mammals, reptiles and insects.

By its consistent destruction of rats and land crabs it does real service to farmers. Flights of termites or white ants are so common before onset of rains, which attracts these foxes.

Its main defenses its speed and its twist and turn. The main breeding season is cold weather. The cubs usually four in number are reared in burrow by both male and female. Gestation period is 50–53 days and cubing time is from February to April.

THE INDIAN WILD DOG
Cuon alpinus (pallas)

Local Name: Dhole, Son Kutta, Jangli Kutta

Size: Height 43–55 cm at the shoulder, Head and body about 90 cm in length, tail 40–43 cm. Big male weight 20 kg, females are lighter (Prater S.H.1980)

Distinctive character: Much like a domestic dog in general appearance, with the long, lanky body of wolf, but relatively shorter in leg and muzzle. Very distinctive is its red coat.

Distribution: Central and eastern Asia, within the limits of India three races are recognized, a Trans -Himalayan, a Himalayan, and a peninsular form.

Habits: Wild Dog keeps entirely in the forest where there is food, shade from the sun and water to drink or lie in; thing wild dogs do in hot weather.

Wild dogs are social animals, going about in packs. The pack is a family of two is more seen in big packs of 40 plus which increases the chances of killing larger prey.

Usually wild dog hunts in day rarely at night. Their prey is various species of deer, large and small. A large pack may attack large animals like gaur and buffaloes but they target calves of these animals. Wild pigs are favorite prey. Panther, bear and even tigers are attacked and killed by wild dog.

There is a myth that wild dog throws its urine through its big tail to prey and big animal like tiger. Also it is said that its urine drops where ever it spreads in the body of prey or any animal acts like acid and skin start rotting, it is not yet confirm but it is believed.

Main breeding season in the peninsular India is between November and December; the majority of cubs, usually 4–6 are born in January and February, in a cave under rock or in an earth. Several females may breed in a colony. The family may unite with other families. These large assemblages are more frequent during the non breeding season i.e. during the hot weather and the rains.

THE STRIPED HYENA
Hyena hyena (Linnaeus)

Local Name: Lakar bagha

Size: Total length of male 5 feet (150 cm); Height about 3 feet (90 cm); weight 38.5 k, females about 4.5 kg less than male (Prater S.H.1980)

Distinctive characters: A dog like build, massive head and fore body, weak hindquarter and a heavy dorsal crest of long hairs. Its colour varies from cream, buff, or tawny to the grey or dirty white. Transverse stripes on body and limbs usually well defined. It is found all over India.

Habits: Hyena is the scavenger of forest feeds on the Caracas of dead animal killed by other carnivores. It eats mostly bones even after Caracas is eaten by vultures after carnivores have eaten its meet.

It is found in low hills and ravines; they come out in night, retiring after sunrise.

THE SLOTH BEARS
Meursus ursinus (Shaw)

Local Name: Bhalu or Reech

Size: Height at Shoulders 65–85 cm, average length 140 to 170 cm. Males usually larger, weighing about 127–145 kg, females 64 kg upwards (prater S.H.1980)

Distinctive Characters: With its elongated muzzle and lower lip, long unkempt hair and short hind legs. Most have a whitish

V shaped breast patch and usually the muzzle and the tips of the feet are dirty white or yellowish. The claws, always longer on the forefeet are ivory white. The coat may have a brownish tinge.

Distribution: The forested Tracks of India and Assam from base of Himalaya to Ceylon.

Habits: Sloth bears live where there is sufficient forest to provide food, and favour places where outcroppings of rocks and tumbled boulders offer them shelter during the hot weather and the rains.

They come out shortly before sunset, hunt for food all night and retire in the morning. In cloudy and cool weather they may be up and about by day.

Their food consists mainly of fruit and insects, but a hungry sloth bear may be driven to eat carrion. Sloth bears is a very hard working animal and had to walk much for food.

Fruits in our jungles are more plentiful in the hot weather. Banyan and other wild figs, mangoes, jambul, bel and ebony trees are all in fruit. This is also the best time for honey. The great combs of the large rock bee, suspended in clusters under rocks or from a branch, and the combs of smaller forest bee usually hidden in tree hollows, are now loaded with honey.

The Bear climbs for fruit, or shakes it down with its great paws. It knocks down a honeycomb and descends to eat it.

In the monsoon, insect food is more plentiful, and bears now find many insects under stones and fallen logs, under bark, and in the crevices of, but their main insect food is termites. Bears are very intelligent and devised method to prick and eat termite by putting a stick inside termite hole and then eating the termites which have come over in stick.

In the cold weather ber trees fruits and later, between March and April, Mowha (Madhuka indica) trees bloom and carpet the ground with heavy scented flowers.

Mating time is usually in the hot weather and most of the young are born seven months later between December and January. The cubs, when sufficiently strong to grip, are carried on the mothers back to and from her feeding grounds. They live with her 2–3 years till they attain maturity. Life spans 40 years approximately.

Sloth Bears, bile found in Gallbladder are priced very high for Chinese traditional medicine and bears are threatened species due to illegal trade of its bile and other animal part.

THE CARACAL

Felis caracal (schreber)

It is called siyeh gosh in Hindi. The caracal has the broad head and tufted ears of the lynx. Like the lynx it stands higher on its hind limbs than on the fore, but it is smaller and lighter in build, has a longer tail. It resembles to lynx.

Its coat though not as dense as that of lynx, is yet thick and soft. The coloring is a uniform reddish grey above fading into buff or white below. Faint indication of spots is presents on the undersurface and sometimes on the back (Prater S.H.1980)

Distribution: Baluchistan, Sindh and cutch. Also found in the drier parts of the Punjab, Rajasthan, Uttar Pradesh and central India.

Habits: An uncommon and elusive animal, fast nearing to extinction in India. I have seen a caracal dead body in Jabalpur Veterinary College brought from Katni - Umariya road must have been killed in by any Vehicle accident in the year 2007–08.

It is the creature of desert and scrub jungle, where it preys on birds, which it is said to take in flight by springing up at them and on rodents, antelope and small deer.

Like cheetah it can be easily tamed and trained to show its ability in hunting small deer, gazelle, hares and foxes, and also birds such as peafowl, crane, and pigeon.

THE GAUR OR INDIAN BISON
Bos gaurus (H.smith)

Size: A bull may stand 6 feet 4 inches (195 cm) at the shoulders. The average is between 5 feet 8 inches and 5 feet 10 inches (180). Female cows are about 4 inches (shorter).Gaur Appear to attain their finest development in the south Indian hill ranges and Assam. Very healthy population of Bison found in central India (Prater S.H. 1980)

The spread of the horns taken together with their girth is the test of a good health. Average Spread 33 inches (85 cm). Cows have smaller, less sturdy horns. An old bull may scale over 900kg.

Distinctive character: With its huge head, deep massive body, and sturdy limbs the Gaur is the embodiment of Vigour and strength, Muscular ridge upon its shoulders which slopes down to the middle of the back where it ends in an abrupt dip.

A newly born Gaur is a light golden yellow which soon changes to fawn, then to light brown and so to coffee or reddish brown, the color of young bulls and cow's. Old bulls are jet black, their bodies almost hairless, An ashy forehead and yellowish -or white stocking.

Distribution: Western Ghats southwards from south Maharashtra, hill forest of central and south eastern peninsula. and west Bengal eastward to Burma and Malaya peninsula.

Habits: Though Gaur come down to low levels at certain seasons in quest of pasture and water they are essentially hill animals.

In hill ranges it climbs to levels of 6000 feet or more but in Himalayas they are seldom found at this height but they mostly remain in foothills.

Forests are essential to the existence of Bison; they like bamboo forest and feed its leaves and twigs. They come out to graze early in the morning and feed till about 9 A.M., or later if the weather is cool and cloudy.

They are in habit of visiting natural salt licks spots where the ground is impregnated with salt and other minerals. Such salt licks are essential for its heath and digestion and it rids of animal from internal parasites.

Gaur is a timid animal and its strength is its size and acute sense of smell, hearing and eyesight are comparatively poor.

The time of mating apparently varies as calves are born at all season's. In M.P. New born are mostly seen from November to March and the peak rut is in March. Gestation period is about 9 months. Mother separates from herd for few days with calf feeding nearby in the vicinity of herds.

Bison are very fond of striping bark of teak in summer for eating as it is having water flowing from phloem and tastes sweet.

WILD BUFFALO
Bubalus bubalis (Linnaeus)

It is called Jangli Bhaisha, Arna (male), Arni (Female).

A large bull stands 5 feet 6 inches at the shoulder and may reach to 6 feet 6 inches (200cm), Weighing 900 kg and above. Head are measured from tip to tip across the fore head. 275 cm is a good head. The record horn measurement is 197 cm (Prater S.H.1980).

Wild buffalo differ little in general appearance from the tame one except perhaps that is sleeker, heavier, and more robust looking. It is also Slaty black. The legs are dirty white upto just above the hocks and the knees.

The new born calf is light colored almost yellow. Wild buffalo exhibits two type of horns one, the horn curve upwards in a semicircle, the tips being separated by a small interval. In the second the horns spread outwards almost horizontally and curve slightly upward and inwards near the tips. Both types may be found in the same herd. The horns are flat and triangular.

Distribution: The Grass jungles of the Nepal, Terai and the plains of the Brahmaputra in Assam, Baster, Sitanadi and Udanti sanctuary. Earlier it was found in Bilashpur in Chhattisgarh and Mandla districts of M.P. in 19th Century.

Habits: Tall grass Jungles and reed brakes in the neighborhood of swamps provide the ideal habitat for buffaloes, offering them both food and shelter, pools of water to lie in and mud wallows in which to roll and cake them with earth. In Sothern dry region with open grass land and tree cover with rivers and nalas.

They feed chiefly on grass, unlike Gaur it can enter cultivated land grazing agriculture crop and it is boldest and may attack without provocation.

Mating is at the end of rains, calves are dropped in March, April and May. Interbreeding with domestic she buffalo may take place occasionally.

THE SPOTTED DEER (CHITAL)

Axis axis

It is called Cheetal in Hindi. In Madhya Pradesh it is at best of growth and population. An adult stag 90 cm at the shoulder and weigh about 85 kg (Prater). Antler on an average is 80 cm. (Prater S.H.1980)

The chital is the most beautiful of all deer, its coat is a bright rufous-fawn profusely spotted with white at all ages and in all season.

Antler have three tine, a long brow tine set nearly at right angles to the beam and two branches tines at the top.

In India Cheetal are found in the forest at the base of Himalayas and practically throughout the peninsula and Ceylon. Where there is jungle combined with good grazing land and plentiful supply of water. It is unknown in the arid plains of the Punjab, large portion of Rajasthan etc.

Chital are seen with beautiful scenery, with grassy forest glades and shaded streams. They are seen in herds of ten to thirty which may contain two are three stags, but assemblages numbering several hundreds have been met with.

They feed late in morning and again in the afternoon and lie down in the interval in some shaded spot.

All stag of deer shade their antlers and time varies, in M.P. it is August and September. The new antlers are in velvet till the end of December. Mating season is April - May. The rutting stag has a loud harsh bellow and combats between the males for the possession of hinds are fierce and frequent. Normally fawns are born in rainy season when there is enough food and tall grasses to hide fawns but we have seen fawn in April and in other months also. one fawn is born but chital is a prolific breeder and in six months may see the production of a new family.

Chital is the main prey of tiger, panther and wild dogs in absence of these they resort to cattle killing.

Their defense is their speed, higher sense of hearing and sighting. They gathered in the open ground in night and sit facing each other so that the group can see all direction for any danger. in summer they stand down a tree where monkeys are sitting to feed on thrown leaves. They are to control grasses and their role is to help natural regeneration of species after eating their fruit and with treated seed in their dung is best to germinate.

Pench Tiger Reserve has a population of more than 40000 in 411 sq km area which is the highest prey base per square km in India

SAMBAR

Cer vus unicolor (Kerr)

It is called Sambar in Hindi, is the largest deer. Height at shoulder nearly 150 cm, a full-grown stag weighs from 225 to 320 kg. (Prater S.H.1980)

Madhya Pradesh has got finest heads in forest area. The coat is coarse and shaggy. General color is brown with a yellowish tinge, females are lighter in tone. Older stags tends to become very dark to almost black. The antlers are stout and rugged. The brow tine is set at an acute angle with the beam. At its summit, the beam forks into two nearly equal tines.

Its habitat is dense forest area found in whole of India.

Forested hill-sides, preferably near cultivation, are the favorite hunt of the Sambar. Their food consists of grass, leaves and various kinds of wild fruit. They feed mainly at night and retire into heavy cover at daybreak and do not usually come out till dusk.

Their powers of sight are moderate, their scent and hearing acute. Sambar takes to water readily and swims with the body submerged.

They shed their horns in April and the horns commence to grow in may and are in velvet during rains and clear of velvet by November by rubbing their horns in a tree. Male stags fight for territory. Mating takes place in November - December. After the rut he deserts them and lives a solitary life till return of mating season. Young stags remain with hinds.

Sambar are rarely seen associating in large numbers, four to dozens are what one usually sees. Both stags and hinds are seen singly or a party of hinds and fawns without a stag.

Sambar is a preferred prey of tiger and if some area is having Sambar population then tiger presence is sure.

BARKING DEER OR MUNT JACK
Muntiacus muntjack

Local Name: Kakar or Bhedki

Size: Height at the shoulder of an adult male is 50–75 cm weight 20 to 25 kg, horn rarely exceeds 5 inches (13 cm) (Prater S.H.1980)

Distinctive Characters: The antlers are small, consisting of a short brow tine and an un branched beam. They are set on bony hair covered pedicels which extends down each side of the face as bony ridges. In do tufts of bristly hair replace the horns?

Old males are browner in colour.

Distribution: Found in greater part of India. In North Indian race colour of coat is bright chestnut.

Habits: The haunts of Muntjack are thickly wooded hills. In the Himalayas and in south India it occur upto levels 5000–8000 feet. They are seen singly or in pairs. Muntjack keep more or less thick jungle and come out to graze in the out skirts of forest or in clearings.

They are fairly diurnal in habit. The food consists of leaves, grasses and wild fruits. The call from a distance sounds much like the bark of a dog. It is given out at intervals usually in the mornings and evenings sometimes after nightfall.

The rut mainly takes place in cold weather. The young ones are born in the beginning of rains. Horns are shed during May and June.

THE INDIAN WILD BOAR

Sus scrofa (Linnaeus)

It is called suar in Hindi

Size: A well grown male stands 90 cm high at the shoulders and its weight may well exceed 230kg. Recorded measurement of lower tusk 32 cm on the outside curve. (Prater S.H.1980)

The Colour of the animal is black mixed with grey, rusty brown and white hairs. The young are browner and old boars greyer. New born wild pigs are brown with light or black stripes. The tushes are well developed in the males. Both the upper and lower tushes curve outwards and project from the mouth.

Wild boars are widely distributed throughout India. It is very common in shrilanka.

Habits: Indian Wild boar live in grass or scanty bush jungle, sometime in forest, after the rains quite commonly found in high crops. They are omnivorous, living on crops, roots, tubers, insects, snakes, offale, and carrion. They feed in the early morning and late in the evening and some time in night. No animal is more destructive to crops and in cultivated areas.

It is plough and plough puller in the forests. Due to its habit of digging earth for root it helps to make soil airy and pulverized which is good for seeds to germinate. Without wild boar forest can become inert and due to lack of regeneration forest may be wiped out.

Wild boar display great intelligence and few animals show greater courage and determination. The sense of smell is acute the eyesight and hearing moderate. Wild boar are highly prolific, they apparently breed on all seasons.

In central India the majority of young are born at two periods, shortly before rains and shortly after the rains. Boars and sows (adult female wild pig) are known to collect in large numbers while pairing, more than 150 numbers may be seen and adult males fighting in central. The period of gestation is four months, 4 to six young are born at a time. The mother shelters them in a heaped-up grass or branches which she builds before she litters.

After breeding the big boars live alone or in company with another of equal size or with one or two sows.

NILGAI OR BLUE BULL

Boselaphus tragocamelus (pallas)

It is called Nilgai, rojh, rojra

Size: Males usually 52–56 inches (130 to 140cm) high may reach to 150 cm. females, much smaller. Average horns length is 8inches (20 cm) (Prater S.H.1980)

Distinctive Characters: A big animal almost horse like in build with high withers and low rump.

The adult bull has a coarse iron grey coat, a white ring below each fetlock and two white spots on each cheek. His lips, chin, the inside of his ears, and the undersurface of his tail are white.

Young bulls and the cows are tawny. Both sexes have dark manes and the male wears a distinctive tuft of stiff black hairs on the throat. The bulls have stout cone like horns.

Distribution: The Nilgai is found only in the Indian peninsula from the base of Himalaya to Mysore. It does not occur in eastern Bengal or Assam.

Habits: Nilgai avoid dense forest. Their usual haunts are hills sparsely dotted with trees, or level or undulating plains covered with grass and patches of scrub.

They freely enters cultivation and are a source of damage to crops. They feed till late in the morning and again early in the evening, caring little about hot sun.

They are both grazer and browser, feeding on leaves and fruits of ber and other trees, very fond of Mahuwa flowers. Nilgai can do for long periods without water and even during hot summer do not drink regularly.

A grunting sound which is alarm cry sends the herd away in the slouching gallop.

Nilgai like antelope have the habit of resorting to the same spot to deposit their droppings forming in this way considerable accommodation mostly in clean path or mid of a road may be keep grazing ground clean.

Four to ten is usual number but may be seen with 20 or more numbers. Young are produced in all seasons; gestation period is 8 to 9 months and female gains sexual maturity at the age of 2 years. One at a time young is born.

Blue Bull is the biggest antelope in Asia. It is most damaging to agricultural crop and fruit crops. Innovative protection method must be used to avoid damage. Thuwar fencing is very effective. Other method of spraying forate insecticide, spraying of phenyl is also effective. People also used excreta of blue bull by spraying it making a solution with water over crop in border area. Audio and video tape is put around field in wooden poles which radiate in the night and blue bull avoids that glittering.

Another cheap method is putting Dummy of men and women made of sticks and old clothes. It distracts blue bull due to presence of farmers in dummy at many places. Ringing of bells in the night is again good prevention. All the night watching by farmers is the best method to ward off the blue bull.

SWAMP DEER OR BARASINGHA
Cervus duvauceli (branderi)

It is called Barasingha in Hindi due to its number of tines to 12 or more.

Size: This splendid deer attains its finest development in M.P. Kanha tiger reserve. A good stag stands 54 inches (135 cm) at the shoulder and weigh 170 to 180 kg. Average horns measures 30 inches (75 cm) with a girth of 5 inches (13 cm)(Prater S.H.1980)

Distinctive Character: The coat, almost wooly in texture, shades from brown to yellowish brown. The stags are maned and darker.

Distribution: Two races are found in India, The swamp dwelling duvauceli of the terai, U.P., Assam and the Sunderbans and branderi found in the hard open ground of Madhya Pradesh.

Habits: In Terai the Barasingha lives on marshland and is seldom out of water but in Madhya Pradesh deer inhabits grassy maidans in the proximity of forest and grazing along side with spotted deer. They feed late in the mornings again in the evening.

Their number has reduced to approximately 400 in Kanha tiger reserve. M.P. forest department has tried to introduce it in Satpuda tiger reserve near Bori adjoining Chhindwara district.

Forsyth has written in his book Highlands of Central India that he has seen a female Barasingha in Delakhari area below Tamia valley which is Sal Forest and inquired from villager that a horn of a stag of Barasingha is kept by an old shikari of the village which shows that Barasingha was found in the Sal forest spreading from Tamia valley toward Pachmadi forest.

FOUR HORNED ANTELOPE (CHOWSINGHA)

Tetracerus Quadricornis (Blainville)

Local Name: Chowsingha

Size: Height of male at shoulder, 25 inches (65 cm). The posterior horns are usually 3 to 4 inches (8–10 cm) long, the inner 0.5 to 1 inches (1 to 2.5 cm)(Prater S.H.1980)

Distinctive characters: This is an antelope in which their horns are not shed and is permanent. But in case of deer horns are shed every year and so they are called antlers. Female is hornless. It has well developed glands between the false hooves of the hind legs in both male and female. The colour of its coarse coat is dull red brown above and white below

Distribution: Peninsular India South of Himalaya in wooded and hilly but not too densely forested area.

Habits: The Chowsingha lives in undulating or hilly country, and shelters in tall grasses and open jungle.

This little animal drinks regularly so they are more found near water. The edge of jungle near village tank is their favorite spots.

The breeding seasons are hot weather and rains and young once are born from October to February. Gestation period is 8 to 8 and half month.

CHINKARA, OR INDIAN GAZELLE
Gazella gazella (Pallas)

Local Name: Hindi- Chinkara.

Size: A full grown male measure about 65 cm at the shoulder and weight about 23 kg (prater, S.H.). The horns averages 10 to 12 inches (25 to 30 cm). The horns of does, usually 10–13 cm (Prater S.H.1980)

Distinctive Characters: A small gazelle of slender graceful build. The body above is light chestnut; under parts white. The horns of the male appear almost straight when seen from the front. They have 15–25 rings. Horns of female smooth, hornless females are not uncommon.

Distribution: The plains and low hills of north western and central India.

Habits: Wastelands broken up by nullahs and ravines, scattered bush and thin jungles are the usual haunts of Chinkara. They are common in the sand hills of the desert zone.

The food consists of grass, various leaves, crops and fruits. They go without water for long periods.

Chinkara are less gregarious than black buck and live in smaller herds. They do not have a particular breeding season but there are two birth peaks the major one in April and a minor one in autumn. Males are territorial demarcated by fecal stations used repeatedly by the male. The gestation period is 5 and half months.

THE BLACK BUCK OR INDIAN ANTELOPE
Antilope cervicarpra

Local Name: Kala hiran or Krishna mriga

Size: A well grown buck stands about 32 inches (80 cm) at the shoulder and average weight 40 kg. Horns seldom exceed 50 cm. (Prater S.H.1980)

Distinctive Characters: The Black Buck is the sole representative in India of the genus Antilope. Its striking colour and its beautiful spiralled horns, which may reach the shoulder height of the animal, give it an elegance hardly equaled by any antelope. This exclusively Indian animal is perhaps the most beautiful of all its kind.

When young its coat like that of the does is a yellowish fawn. When three years old it commences to turn black. Horned females are occasionally but rarely met with. Female attains sexual maturity between the age of 19 to 23 months.

Distribution: Black buck used to occur in practically all the plains Except along the Indian Coast southward from the neighborhoods of Surat They avoid Forest and Hill tracks.

Habits: Blacks are usually seen in herds of 20–30 though in Rajputana and the Punjab gatherings may number several hundreds. These antelopes live in open plains covered with scrub or cultivation. They enter open forests which contain wide expenses of grass.

They feed on grass and various cereal crops. Usually Black bucks graze till near noon and again in the late afternoon lying down to rest during the hot hours of the day. Their senses of hearing is moderate, scent fair. Keen eye sight and speed are their protection. When alarmed the herd moves off in a series of light leaps and bounds and then breaks into gallop.

The leadership of herd is by vigilant female. Black buck breeds in all seasons but the main rut takes place between February and March when the bucks fight each other for the possession of the does, one or two young's are produced at a time.

Black bucks have become destructive for Soybean crop and hens a major Man animal conflict issue in Madhya Pradesh, Seoni, Chhindwara, Sagar etc districts, But it was a boon to farmers when they were cultivating Horse gram because production of horse gram is manifold due to nibbling of branches of horse gram crop which produces more branches and hens more production.

Tigress with Cub: Photo by R. G. Soni

Territory marking by Tiger: Photo by Jagdish Chandra

Leopard: Photo by Jagdish Chandra

Wolf: Photo by R. G. Soni

Jackal: Photo by R. G. Soni

Fox

Wild Dog on hunting: Photo by Jagdish Chandra

Wild Dog: Photo by Jagdish Chandra

Wild Dog: Photo by R. G. Soni

Striped Hyena

Sloth Bear

Sloth Bear

Caracal

Indian Bison: Photo by R. G. Soni

Indian Bison: Photo by R. G. Soni

Wild Buffalo

Spotted Deer: Photo by R. G. Soni

Sambar: Photo by Jagdish Chandra

Sambar: Photo by R. G. Soni

Barking Deer

Barking Deer

Wild boar: Photo by R. G. Soni

Wild boar: Photo by Jagdish Chandra

Nilgai (Blue Bull): Photo by R. G. Soni

Swamp Deer: Photo by Jagdish Chandra

Four Horned Antelope: Photo by R. G. Soni

Chinkar a: Photo by R. G. Soni

Black Buck: Photo by Jagdish Chandra

Chapter 5

MANAGERIAL EFFECTIVENESS IN PROTECTION OF WILD LIFE

Manager of a National park, tiger reserve, sanctuary or territorial forest division Should be aware of the threat to his wild animals from poachers and need of the wild animals to survive in that habitat.

THERE ARE FOLLOWING IMPORTANT ISSUES NEED TO BE TACKLED

Poaching

Poaching of wild animal can happen inside park or in buffer area. Manager should gather information from past cases from staff and from other sources. He should find out various community living in the vicinity of the park and their behavior specially if Pardi or other hunting tribes are living nearby he should be more cautious and should keep watch on the activity of these communities by strong network of informers.

Pardis are so clever a cast that killing a tiger is as simple as plucking a Pumpkin from his vegetable garden is the narration for Pardis by then D.F.O. Katni Mr. Chitranjan Tyagi, which is the district where they have permanent houses and they all come in holi festival.

Park manager should have strong informer network to know movement of Pardis in his area and check them so that they do not stay there.

Pardis had very cordial relations with villagers especially rich because they were regularly called by them to get rid of tiger if operating in that area and doing cattle lifting since ages. They also help to kill wild boar and deer for farmers to save crop.

Success lies in timely information and better liaison with local public and timely distribution of compensation of cattle kill.

Parad or Group hunting by Tribal community

In Tribal areas they have their custom of group hunting during some festival time especially if tribal has previous records of that then you should know it how to check. When group hunting is done? And which festival time it happens so that either you convince them or check them by force.

We must analyze at least 10 year data of wild life related crime from this area and adjoining forest division. He must read Gazetteer of the district and any other books of the area to find out old practices of wild life crime.

Electrocution:-

Lot of animal are killed by electrocution some time they put naked wire inside forest area by putting small wooden stick of 6–8 inches and it is always across path of wild animals or water holes and is spread for kilometers upto Power line passing through forest.

They temporality put a wire to live electrical line having power and it is then connected to ground wire they have spread.

It is guarded by them and any animal crossing the path will electrocuted by that.

For this you must know vulnerable areas and you should direct staff for regular patrolling. Also keep a liaison with electricity Deptt especially local staff should talk to line man of these areas. If there is tipping of the line due to electrocution of animal then electricity Deptt. Can tell the location immediately and our staff can apprehend culprits.

Other areas are farmer's fields adjoining forest area where wild animals go for grazing of crop and carnivores go for killing cattle. We have to tell farmers not to do that reminding of them legal punishment for crime against wild animals.

POISONING OF WILD ANIMALS

Poisoning in waterholes

Poisoning is done by poachers by putting poison in small waterholes. Water holes are to be regularly checked by staff and daily wage employee posted in the area. Apart from herbivores even tiger die due to this. We should be careful in regular patrolling of waterholes.

Poisoning in dead body of cattle killed by carnivores

If tiger and panther kill the cattle of villagers then out of anger they put poison in dead body resulting in death of tiger or panther after eating his kill. We have to be alert and ensure to distribute compensation of cattle to the owner within a week so that they do not poison the kill and our tiger is safe. This is possible only if you take help of cattle herders and use them as informer by paying some reward.

Pardi community and poaching

Pardi community is responsible for 90% of poaching of tiger and panther. They do poaching in all national parks, sanctuary, and tiger reserve and in buffer area throughout India and go to Nepal. This tribe is of two measure clan one is Haryanvi and the other is Gujrati. They have a common place to come in festival of Holi in Katni district where they come every year but they don't live permanently.

We must know about Pardis their culture, habit, tradition and way of hunting.

It is said that if Pardi stay in an area for a week where tiger is their then poaching a tiger in that area is as easy as to pluck a pumpkin from your kitchen garden. They usually sell Kesar of Kashmir and some Ayurvedic medicine. They are very wise and know the habit of tiger so they can find out the movement of tiger and they put iron trap kiss crossing the path so that tiger foot is trapped in iron trap and it cannot remove. They watch it from a distance sitting in a tree and then they come and insert the bamboo in his mouth so tiger die and with in no time they properly take out the skin, bone and all body parts out. They dry the skin and fold in a proper way and this is kept by Pardi women wrapped around her waist under her cloth so that nobody can check it.

Pardis were commanding respect and good relations from village community because they help them to kill tiger, panther that kill their cattle and also they help to kill wild boar and blue bull that do crop raiding. So Pardis have local support by which they get all information about tiger movement. They could get information about cattle kill by tiger and then they plan out poaching of tiger as tiger remain there for 2–3 days with the kill.

It can only be checked if we have effective network of informers.

For effective control on poaching you have to resort to such informer system which can prevent wildlife crime or at least help to catch criminal so that further crime is controlled.

PROTECTION MEASURE

One such measure is giving reward to person who gives information about crime and poachers. Reward can be given from Van surksha purskar niyam. This can be done by publicity in print media or electronic media as to whom they should give information by telephone or mobile phone.

You can give information to public by putting poster at public offices, range office, depot office, Panchayat office, Gram sabha etc. You have to write as to whom they should give information about crime or for preventing wild life crime like telling about people going for hunting in forest etc and how much reward they will get without disclosing his /her name.

I have applied this system with very successful result. People have differences and you have to get benefit out of this for good of wildlife. This is very simple and handy as you cannot have so much staff to know information of all area.

Another way to effectively check the wild animal poaching is to make record of all cattle herders (Charwahas) bringing cattle in buffer area for grazing and telling them to report any kill by tiger, panther or movements of poachers in that area. As they are there for whole day they are effective informer of wild life crime. You can award them for their information from "van surksha purskar niyam".

You have to efficiently check the hunting of herbivores and poaching of carnivores for proper and effective wild life management and this can only be possible if you apply above mentioned measures. Then you can say that I am doing management without tears, otherwise I have seen officers running pillar to post without proper management techniques.

Chapter 6

MAN ANIMAL CONFLICT AND MANAGEMENT EFFECTIVENESS

Man and animal conflict is a serious problem these days and management has to deal it effectively for protection of wildlife.

Most common conflict is killing of cattle by carnivores.

CATTLE KILL AND EFFICIENT DISTRIBUTION OF COMPENSATION

Tiger kill constitute 20 to 30% of cattle kill especially by those tigers which are living in buffer area or which are old and survived only on cattle prey. Panther mostly active between forest and village, they mostly kill goat and sheep but also kill cattle.

Wolves are also active in villages and kill Sheep and goats.

Tiger and panther kills cattle and is cause of concern to management, because villagers suffer heavy losses due to cattle kill and so they tend to become hostile and put Aldrin an insecticide into dead body of cattle. Tiger and panther normally eat their prey for 2–3 days so cattle owner or poachers pour the Aldrin in dead body of cattle so eating poisoned kill they die due to poison.

Villagers take help of hunters, poachers and Pardis to illuminate carnivores which kill their cattle. This is a dangerous situation and we can lose tiger and panther which are already in danger.

Many tiger reserve has become tiger less and tigers are in danger in other parks and wild animal areas due to poaching.

EFFECTIVE WAY OF DEALING CATTLE KILL AND CONFLICT

I would like to tell a case study where we were successful in dealing with this issue very efficiently.

There was a tigress in Pench tiger reserve having 4 cubs in the year 2002–03 and active in buffer zone in Chhindwara District and it used to kill 2–3 cattle daily to feed their growing cubs. Though this tigress was from Alikatta range where there is no dearth of spotted deer but for the safety of their cubs she has gone to buffer area for two reasons one to save cubs from male tiger and another to kill cattle which are easily available.

There was danger of putting Aldrin poison by villagers if we could not act in time. People of the area were agitated as tigress was killing their cattle.

So I devised an idea which is as follows. I told our staff to record name of all cattle herder grazing their cattle in the area where tigress is operating and tell all Charwahas that once tigress kills their cattle they should not disturb the kill but send one of their person to nearest forest staff and tell all details of where the tigress has killed the cattle and name of the owner of the cattle.

Our staff will give wireless message to his higher officer and they will convey it to deputy director and Field director. Local staff has to pay 500 rupees as van surksha purskar reward to the Charwahas giving information. If information is given on second day he will be paid 300 rupees only and any delay afterwards will be seen as his act of defiance and he may be barred from grazing in buffer area.

Then our staff should see that all the formalities of making compensation case is completed within fortnight and full payment of compensation has to be ensured in time. This will help to win-win situation where owner of the cattle is not annoyed and this will save our tiger.

HUMAN DEATH AND INJURY BY CARNIVORES

This happens when people go to forest to collect fuel wood, Tendu patta or any other forest produce. Sometimes our tiger, panther comes out of forest in villages and they accidently or otherwise injure or kill human being then local staff must arrange for treatment and give some amount immediately as token gesture for his /her treatment or for rituals in case of death then ensure full payment as per guidelines of the Deptt., In time and with ease.

Manager should see that people are properly guided as to how they should behave and protect themselves from wild life in forest area.

CROP RAIDING BY HERBIVORES

It is very important cause of conflict with villagers and should be dealt with human angle. There are various ways to deal with this conflict including creating awareness about wildlife and how to save their crop.

DIRECT METHOD TO PREVENT AND COMPENSATE CROP LOSS

1. Cattle proof wall:

This was very successful in Pench tiger Reserve Seoni M.P., where we have built CPW (cattle Proof Wall) out of boulders 2 Mt High, 2.5 Mt breadth at bottom, one meter breadth at top in the border of villages adjoining core area of PTR. This can be made 8 feet high. This helped to save adjoining crop of farmers and they started sowing crops which they were left untilled due to fear of grazing by wild animals.

This is always not possible due to vast forest tracts, but we can do where ever possible.

2. Other Management tools:

Govt. has made rules to compensate loss of crop by farmers and this can be very easily done and we must help poor farmers so that we have good relation with locals which will help save wildlife.

INDIRECT METHOD THROUGH PERSUADING PEOPLE TO SAVE THEIR CROP

Farming in adjoining forest areas need round the clock surveillance without which you cannot protect crop. Night watcher is a must to keep away wild animals grazing their crop. But since farmers have the knowledge when it is more vulnerable to be strictly guarded and when not so, they adjust accordingly.

Few case studies relating to crop grazing by wild animals and remedy prescribed for that.

1. Black Buck problem in Seoni District of M.P. and Remedy suggested:-

Thousands of black buck roam in an area of around 50000 hectares and people were complaining of crop raiding by black buck and they were putting political pressure to either capture them or they will be kept in an enclosure.

Issue was raised before forest minister who happens to be from that area and Principal Chief Conservator of forest told me to find out solution for that.

I went to the area and inquired and found that farmers started cultivating soya been and this crop is damaged due to browsing. But in old time farmers were cultivating horse gram which is squarely benefited by browsing of black buck and production is fourfold, but due to change in crop those black buck who were beneficial for crop became nuisance. So we ignorantly curse the black buck who was there since ages though it is our fault.

This was brought to the knowledge of important persons of the area and peoples were told to change crop as was done by their forefathers.

2. Problem of wild boar in crop destruction:

Wild boar is a greater menace for crop raised near forest having wild boar population especially for Rice crop.

There was an old saying in Hindi

"Dhan boye Kardhi Na suar khaye Na Samadhi"

If you sow Kardhi rice it will not be eaten by wild boar and because it is red color it will not be served to father in law of your son /daughter means by your respected guest. But Kardhi rice is full of nutrient and gives good yield again this is in great demand now days by rich people who want to eat coarse millet which is a healthy diet.

Wild boar is very important for regenerating forest as it helps to dig soil and make soil porous during course of his eating habit. He eats root of plant, tuber etc for that it actually did tilling of soil as is done by farmers by plough to make his farms fertile.

So the wild boar is plough and the puller both. We cannot manually or by tractor plough our vast forest tracks but wild boar does this naturally. So people wanting to kill wild boar has to adjust by changing the crop or otherwise.

Wild animals are there for the benefit of forest and they are not unwanted, the problem is that we have to adjust and learn from our old practices which are helpful to both.

Tribal use to cultivate Kodo and Kutki a variety of course millet used like rice and it is not eaten by wild animals and a short rotation crop, very nutritious and now a day's much preferred by rich people as healthy diet. Earlier it was eaten by poor people so it was selling very cheap but due to its demand by large number of people with high income group so it is advisable to invent cropping of these grains in tribal areas near protected areas.

3. Problem of grazing by spotted dear and other wild animals in a village Karmajhiri just adjacent to Pench tiger reserve Seoni M.P.

I have seen this that villagers were cultivating Maize which was eaten away by spotted deer in the night. But we constructed stop dam for irrigation along with bunding of their farms under Govt. scheme resulted in bumper crop of wheat which they protected in night. They said wheat needs protection in early month and once it become coarse it is not eaten so they could learn the method to survive with bumper crop they could do it.

Again due to increase tourism their income has increased and with more income their grievances were solved on their own.

4. Wild animal's population is balanced through Prey -Predator equation:-

Prey-predator equation balances each other population in undisturbed environment but it is shattered by human intervention like poaching of either prey or predator species.

In Maharashtra wild boar population increased due to absence of leopard and tiger and they were doing extensive damage to sugar cane field and other agriculture crop as per study carried out in that area.

Similarly blue bull population increases due to absence of tiger and panther. So if we want to check such menaces we have to bear with the presence of tiger and panther.

Every wild animal has its roll to balance each other and are important for the very health of forest. Tiger is at the apex of food chain and its presence signifies the good health of the ecosystem.

It is very common now a days that if a tiger is spotted in a forest area adjoining any village and it kills few cattle being its prey lot of hue and cry by public is seen and our Deptt., in place of making them aware as to how it is natural and compensating promptly try to capture the tiger and send it to other distant location, which is not the correct remedy to solve man animal conflict.

In good olden days in British time there were lot of wild life including tigers but people knew how to deal with the wild animals and they don't put pressure on Deptt. But in political system no body want to annoy public and our staff has no knowledge as to how they should be told or behave in case of presence of tiger in the area.

In the past people at the point of entry of forest they had Tiger statue called Bagh baba and they worship and then inter into forest. This is to say that they have respect for tiger and know that it has to live there but we have to learn how to make sure that they return safely. In case of accident where tiger killed someone or hurt any person it was treated as God act and they don't have any enmity to tiger. This was a great tradition to live and let live other creatures of God in their area.

But this has eroded due to our fault by not making them aware of the habits of wild animals and their importance for forest conservation and mankind.

Tiger is a gentle wild animal and it never attacks unless you came upon him suddenly and in his safety it attacks human being otherwise if you move inside forest doing some noise either by loud voice or by beating the stick in the road tiger, will move away without attacking you. Similarly you have to make noise to save you from panther and move in a group beating the stick in the road.

There can only be attack by tiger or panther if they are man eater and they have tasted the blood of human otherwise they will not attack if you move as told above.

I would like to narrate one instance when I was field director Pench tiger reserve when members of estimate committee of legislative assembly visited this area and I interacted with them that our assembly has passed a law to kill wild boar if it inters Pvt. fields, and shown them group of wild boar and its role as plough and plough puller to make forest soil fertile by digging roots of plants.

Without wild boar our forest will not regenerate hence they are very important for ecosystems, they agreed and told me that they did not know the work done by wild boar in preserving forest. So the point is that unless we tell the people the importance of wild life and contribution of each species people being ignorant will not save them.

This is the best technique to first understand the roll of each species in conservation and regeneration of flora and then properly communicate this knowledge to public in large through publicity by print and electronic media.

4. Sowing of Crop which is not damaged by wild animals in farms near Wild areas:

Crop selection near forest and wild animal menace area is very important for villagers to survive in farming near Forest. Our Forefathers were very intelligent and has knowledge of thousands of years as what is to be sown in these wild and forest areas.

They know since ages which crop ripens in less time and which is not eaten by wild boar and other herbivores.

Earlier tribal used to sow Kodo and Kutki which comes out in 60 days and no need of irrigation or extra water. They even don't till the farm but broadcast seeds of kodo, kutki in lands which is unfertile land called bhatar (Bhata or usher land). This crop is not grazed or destroyed by any wild animals and it is very rich in nutrient, fat free full of calcium etc. It is a variety of Rice and eaten like rice by poor people. Kodo and Kutki seeds can be stored for 100 years and not spoiled.

We can market it by publicity and can get price more than Rice in the name of organic food and healthy diet.

Similarly some variety of Rice like Kardhi etc can be cultivated near forest area to save them from wild animals.

OUT OF BOX WAY OF DEALING WITH MAN ANIMAL CONFLICT

1. Cure of Malaria by Medicinal Plant:

There were 100 odd villages adjoining to buffer area of Pench Tiger reserve and Malaria fever were rampant specially during rainy season and cost of cure through allopath was very high and every year per family average cost was rupees 2000/-3000/ and sometimes death were reported. People living in remote area were poor and there is no proper hospital.

This problem was solved by me by advising them to take quath of kalmegh (Andrographis penniculata) plant for a month in rainy season which will prevent any type of fever and it is cure as well.

Procedure: - To make quath you have to boil 50 gram of dried kalmegh plant (called panchang) in one liter of water till it is left with one fourth of water, it is called quath. After cooling of this Quath for prevention one has to take half a cup approx.20–30 ml every morning before taking breakfast for at least 15 days but for better results for a month. This will prevent all type of fever including dengue, chikenguniya, and typhoid.

For cure same dose has to be taken twice, once in morning and in the evening for one month and for children below 5 yrs half the dose will be sufficient.

As kalmegh plant is there in the forest they can use it and I told them that if you burn our forest this species along with many valuable medicinal plants will be destroyed forever and your future generation will be deprived of this and will suffer for want of medicine.

Earlier forest fire were very rampant and it was manmade but once they were told about the importance of forest and medicinal plants found in the forest and after they were cured and had full belief in this plant there were zero fire in the park.

This was the best goodwill approach to win over public favour to solve man animal conflict and which helped a lot for protecting our wild life.

This prescription was also used by our staff and daily wagers doing camp duty and were free of malaria and other fever otherwise one third of staff used to be ill and on leave suffering badly in health and money.

This is out of box thinking to solve man animal conflict and to gain favour from local people for conservation of wild life.

2. Distributing food grains to Poor household in surrounding villages during summer:-

Approximately 60% population of 100 odd villages were below poverty line and they don't have enough money to have meals in rainy season because there is no work in that time so they take money as a loan every year from big farmers or money lenders with high rate of interest or to work in their farm with low wages which is half of the prevailing rate.

This was a great plight of poor villagers then I introduced a plan of food grain bank in which we have authorized eco development committee to purchase rice from their welfare money to distribute at least one quintal rice per family or more according to the size of family.

This helped a lot and they got double the wages and their proud was not compromised. They have to return the rice after their crop is harvested with 10% more rice and will be kept with chairman of Eco committee to be distributed again during summer or whenever there is a need for any family.

This way food grain bank will rotate year after year to help poor villagers and in turn they help us in conservation of wildlife and protection of our forest from fire and illegal felling. They also help as informer to tell about hunters and poachers and any new person entering our forest by informing us.

These are the welfare schemes to win over the confidence of local villagers and help to solve man animal conflict.

Cattle proof wall: Photo by R. G. Soni

Kalmegh Plant (Andrographis penniculata): Photo by R. G. Soni

Chapter 7

HUMAN RESOURCE AND ITS MANAGEMENT

Success of an organization depends on the spirit of its employs, motivation, dedication and commitment to the target of its organization.

Forest and wildlife staff posted in national park and sanctuaries mostly lives in remote areas and without their families and children due to lack of educational facilities.

In the past lower rank guard and forester were from villages and less educated did not find much difficulty in living in remote forest posts, but new generation recruit are highly educated so they do not find it comfortable to live in remote area which lacks basic facilities of electricity, hospital etc.

Here comes the role of leader who is in charge of protected area to educate them and appreciate the work and its importance.

Wildlife manager should have adequate knowledge of the wildlife its habits in his area so that he can develop interest in them and engage them in some or the other observational research and interact with them, give credit and appreciation to deserving staff so that others also follow.

Human resource management is a new tool and is a subject in Master of business administration. Success of an organization largely depends upon how best you manage your subordinates.

Success of a manager or a leader depends upon some of the following characteristics behavior:-

CHARACTER ISTIC QUALITY OF A LEADER

1. Leader should treat all his subordinate with equality:
Leader should be unbiased as to cast, religion, native of subordinate but give credit to hard working, dedicated staff so that others should also fall in line to perform better.

2. Leader must have adequate knowledge of his profession and work he has to do:
Leaders having adequate and perfect knowledge of their work can motivate his subordinate better as compared to leader having little knowledge of the subject.

3. Leader should himself be hardworking and positive towards his work:
If you are not a hard task master you cannot extract work from your subordinate.

4. Leader should be aware of the problems of his staff and try to solve if possible by him:
Wild life staff is posted in remote areas and they are likely to fall ill due to fever, diarrhea etc. so we should advice to keep first adds treatment. Management should know and help them.

5. Dues, pay and T.A., promotion and posting of staff should be taken care off:
Normally staff is posted in remote areas and they don't have time to see that his pay, DA,T.A., arrears is paid in time and staff should know that his higher authority are taking care of his or her interest.

6. Allotment of duty to different staff should be done on the basis of ability of subordinate:

Management should know all his subordinate and their plus and minus point so as to decide the duty to be given to particular staff looking to the overall benefit of the organization.

7. Award and punishment:

This is the most important tool to motivate better staff and discourage bad staff.

We must appreciate the work done by our subordinate and give award or recommend to state for Gold medal or out of turn promotion if the work is extra ordinary, this will motivate others to do good work.

I as field director Pench tiger reserve recommended one forest Guard named Gautam Soni for out of turn promotion for his work of making a small jhiriya in a forest where there was no water and this jhiriya retained water for whole of summer. He was promoted to forester by State Government.

There was acute shortage of water in Pench and this resulted in all staff and chaukidars started searching for natural source of water and we had 100s of such water bodies.

Most of the tiger reserve, national park and sanctuaries have acute shortage of water and this type of innovative idea has played immense role in the success of wild life management.

OTHER PROBLEMS OF WILD LIFE AREAS

1. Malaria fever problem in wild area:

In remote forest areas malaria fever is rampant and most of the staff suffer from this which adversely affect protection due to absence of such staff who are ill. This also put unnecessary financial burden on staff. So it is essential to help them with meditational support and medical bill reimbursement.

I have introduced a medicinal plant called Kalmegh (Andrographis penniculata) decoction of its dried powder prevents malaria. 50 gram dried powder is boiled in one liter of water till one fourth water is remaining, 20 ml of this quath is taken in the morning for one month in the month of July - August when malaria fever is specially occur in more intensity. This dose prevents malaria and if somebody has malaria fever then 20 ml morning and evening both time has to be taken for cure.

We used to distribute one packet of Kalmegh (200 gram) to each staff and it is available in the forest so they can use it fresh plant once they are told and identified. This helped our staff to be healthy.

2. Snake bite and other ailments:

Snake bite is quite common in forest area and in Protected areas anti venom has to be kept in advance to save the life of staff. Precautionary practices are told to everybody and first aid kit is very important to be kept there with every staff.

In case of emergency vehicle should be there to help staff to shift to nearby hospital.

EXTRA BENEFITS TO BE GIVEN TO STAFF POSTED IN WILDLIFE AREA

In Madhya Pradesh, one month extra pay was given in PA areas from the fund collected by entree fees. But this should be given to all forest staff by Govt., because they live in remote areas and living in difficult situation and maintain two accommodation one for himself and another for family in town area.

Govt. should provide living accommodation to children of employees in town areas.

It is high time Govt. of India should provide free ration to forest Deptt. upto deputy ranger in order to help staff posted in remote areas to save wild life.

State govt. should provide rapid action force with vehicle to check poaching to each range and motorcycle to each guard and forester.

It is high time that govt. should provide arms to field staff along with license to use it.

Looking to high illegal trade in wild life just like narcotics it should be equipped in that line in order to stop poaching in present scenario.

Chapter 8

EFFECTIVE CONTROL OF BUFFER AND VILLAGES INSIDE

Tiger reserve is declared under section 38 V (1) of wild life protection act 1972 as amended in 2006 on the recommendation of state government by Central Government.

It has core and buffer area. Core or critical tiger area is managed for the tiger and wildlife whereas Buffer is an area adjoining core /critical tiger habitat and is multiple use area. Buffer area is notified as an area for fanning out population of tiger but here all forestry operation are being carried out along with allowing grazing and collection of non wood forest produce for livelihood concern of people living in and around buffer.

Now every tiger reserve has been notified along with buffer and it is in control of Wildlife wing of forest department. Tiger reserve may be sanctuary or National park.

When we say that wildlife manager has to exercise full control of buffer area then we also say that apart from administrative control of the area we must see that habitat of buffer should have enough water holes and grassland so that it can keep tigers and wild life coming to this area and their protection from poaching.

[If we could protect buffer we can increase tiger population.]

Village inside buffer and adjoining area need not be relocated unless they are willing or if some village is secluded or it is in remote area. Buffer is multiple use area and cattle population is utilized as prey as 20 to 30% of tiger kill is of cattle.

Villages inside core area may be relocated with the consent of villagers but some villages may not be relocated as they have balanced with the system and their cattle will be prey to tiger as tiger prey has 20 to 30% cattle, so removing village will result in less prey and tiger has to move towards buffer villages.

This has been observed in Gir National Park where by removing Maldhari camps from core area lions shifted to sanctuary area having Maldhari camps.

Annual cattle kill reported from Gir National Park of Gujarat are 4500 to 5000 and they pay annual compensation approximately in the range of 5–6 crores of rupees.

Instead of thinking villages as enemy to wild life we can educate them and compensate them for loss of cattle.

VILLAGE RELOCATION

Enormous Money is spend in relocation of core and Buffer villages and this has been seen as the most useful work to be done. M.P. has spend nearly 500 crores of rupees in 4–5 years in relocation of villages where as total money spent for actual wild life management may be less than 10% annually if you exclude staff salary.

Govt. should allocate at least 25% of budget out of relocation fund to be utilized in restoring relocated villages and other core and buffer areas and emphasis should be to spend money on proper wild life management first then go for village relocation if at all needed and budget should be asked for habitat management which should not be less than village relocation budget, rather village relocation budget must include 25% money for restoration of relocated villages.

Past experience in M.P. shows that though villages have been relocated successfully but village land were not restored to attract spotted deer and other herbivore due to lack of palatable grasses and water.

Villagers should be helped in their endeavor for proper crop which is not grazed by wild life or by constructing cattle proof wall or stone wall to save their crop. Villagers can be trained in ecotourism for their livelihood.

Tourism in buffer area will enhance ecotourism and also protection of wild life in buffer area due to increase presence of staff. Increase tourism helps employment in rural area.

As I have narrated in the Chapter of man animal conflict we have to apply out of box thinking like prevention and cure of malaria fever and establishment of food grain bank etc.

ESTABLISHMENT OF CAMPS AT SUITABLE PLACES

Prior to formation of Buffer, the area was managed as forest area in beats and it is sometimes consists of 5–10 compartment from 3000 hectares to 6000 hectares and was looked after by one beat guard but due to vulnerability of wild life and to rule out poaching we have to have more camps at strategic locations and 3–4 daily wage chaukidars along with one game guard has to be posted with wireless facility, This will help the protection of wildlife in buffer area as this is more vulnerable than core area.

Villagers should be made informer and we should do it secretly so that his identity is not open and he informs about movement of outsiders.

Chapter 9

DEVELOPMENT OF HABITAT IN BUFFER AREA FOR FANNING OUT POPULATION

Development of habitat of buffer area is very essential to sustain fanning out population of tiger and other wild animals.

Major requirement of wild life are water availability round the year and good grassland and surrounding dense forest.

Water: Water is the most important thing to retain tiger and other prey animals. Tiger needs lot of water and our forest does not have water source due to sandy soil, it is found in sub soil 4–6 feet below the ground at some places which can be made available by digging small jhiriyas.

You did not see most of the wild animals in areas which does not have enough water.

We have already discussed as to how we can have various structures to retain water like small tanks, solar tube well, jhiriyas, Dykes, stop dams etc.

CONSTRUCTION OF SOIL STOP DAM/CHECK DAM, IN SMALL NALAS

In October -November you must stop water by check damming small nalas at 1–2 km interval by black cotton soil and core of it should have black cotton soil after pudlling.

Waste weir should be given from one side. This will retain water till April and then you can dig small jhiriya down below which will last till summer. The place of check dam should be identified and you have to construct it every year as it cost very less amount but it is very useful not only as water whole but also lot of grasses will come up for grazing. It is utilized by various animals. Wild boars used it for mud bath and Sambar for wallowing in December during mating season.

Care should be taken that we must have water in summer otherwise wild life will not rely on the area and will migrate to other areas.

All we have to do is to construct small tank in a nala which will retain rain water and if needed a solar tube well can be installed to have sufficient water till summer. Water availability will ensure spotted dear, wild boar, Sambar and tiger.

So it is essential to make buffer conducive for fanning out wild life population.

Grass land improvement: There may not be proper grassland with palatable grasses or the area may have weed growth or small shrubs or it may have under stocked area, in that case we have to eradicate lantana and other weeds and uproot shrubs.

Area should be ploughed by heavy plough and weeds etc are removed. Palatable grass seeds should be spread along with seeds of some important legumes.

All works of pastureland development work should be done, area should be fenced by wire mess and pastureland should be maintained for three years, if possible solar tube well should be established which will serve for irrigating the pasture as well as water source for drinking water to wild animals. Small ponds can be made to store rainy water as well as water from tube well in summer.

After three years fencing will be removed and this will be utilized elsewhere. Pasture land of at least 10 hectare should be developed at 3–5 kilometer radius depending upon availability of such areas.

Chief wild life warden are empowered to prescribe habitat improvement in an area he thinks suitable for it. It has been seen that chief wild life wardens do not exercise this power which is very important for increase in prey base.

Salt Licks: There may not be natural salt licks in the area so we can put man made salt lick bricks near water wholes, it will be very useful for prey base population to increase.

Planting or showing of Ber (Zijuphus jujuba) etc: It is advisable to plant ber shrub either by plant or by showing seeds of local ber which will come up in 2–3 years and is very useful for spotted deer and sambhar.

Planting of Tree and bamboo: If Buffer forest is sparse then we can create pockets of dense tree stand or bamboo clumps which acts as hiding places for carnivores to ambush their prey. This dense crop also helps as resting place for tiger etc.

You can also plant Bargad (Ficus bengalensis) plant at some places which is useful to provide shed to wild animals in summer and in hot day time. Some fruit bearing forestry species like Khamer (Gmelina arborea) etc and good fodder species like Kasai, saja may be planted.

If buffer area is developed on above lines then this can be as good as core area and will sustain fanning out population

Chapter 10

INFORMER NETWORK AND ITS UTILIZATION FOR PREVENTION OF WILD LIFE CRIME

Use of informer is crucial to prevent the crime against wild animals. Police also keeps number of informers to check crime. Police have kotwar in each revenue village whose duty is to report any crime or any information relating to crime directly to police.

In PA areas one beat guard controls approximately 30 sq km area and there are some camps in sensitive areas but poachers can sneak into forest as these guards and camp staff are mostly barefoot.

We have to devise efficient informer's network and coordination of all agencies has to be taken for strengthening the system.

CHARWAHAS NETWORK (CATTLE HERDER)

Cattle grazing is allowed in buffer areas which surrounds core area of PA and cattle of surrounding villages graze their cattle in specified compartments allotted for villages. We have to list all the cattle herders grazing their cattle herds, their names, addresses and we have to enroll them as our informer as they are grazing their cattle in our forest area.

Char wahas are present in forest from morning till evening so they know the movements of our tiger, panther and deer etc. They can tell if any poacher or persons belonging to such community involve in hunting like Baheliya, Pardi etc. have entered into forest.

They are also utilized as informer for cattle kill to save tiger by promptly distributing compensation to the owner of cattle.

This was successfully used as an effective system to avoid man animal conflict and for fast and efficient distribution of cattle compensation.

Char wahas of buffer villages were told to report cattle kill immediately to nearest forest staff if their cattle is killed by tiger without disturbing the tiger. If he reports same day then he will get 500 rupees,for second day report 300 rupees and if he did not report or reports after second day he will be black listed and will not be allowed to graze.

After getting information from him forest staff will have to do everything for making compensation to the owner within fortnight so that anonymity in public does not prevail.

This helped to save a tigress having four cubs by promptly distributing the compensation and giving rewards to informers. Charwahas list should be also prepared in adjoining forest areas and they should be enrolled as informers by local staff.

KOTWAR

Kotwar can be made informers of adjoining villages and our local staff should keep in touch with them to seek information about hunters of these villages.

OTHER INFORMERS

Officers and subordinate staffs on their own wisdom should have number of informers whom they can pay on regular basis and whose identity should not be disclosed.

We can follow the police system and payment can be done under Van surksha purskar niyam.

GENERAL INFORMERS CREATED BY GIVING REWARD

This is very effective in modern day mobile network availability in remote areas. You have to give publicity for reward to be given to those who help to catch poachers, hunters indulge in hunting of wild animal or even before they commit the crime in position of preparedness to hunt any wild animal which is crime under wildlife protection act 1972. A group of hunters going for hunting in forest can be caught before they actually killed any wild animal in the forest sitting to kill. This information is more useful than after wild animal already hunted.

Care should be taken to tell that their identity will not be disclosed and money paid by Boucher will not show informers name.

Publicity can be done through news papers, electronic media, social networking etc by properly mentioning mobile numbers of concern officers and amount of reward.

In villages people have differences and even neighbors can be bitter enemy, so you have to use all these tactics to catch the offenders and control poaching of wild animals.

I have used this when i was posted as conservator of forest Chhindwara circle in 2005–2007 with great success. People have given live information of hunting and transporting killed animal and culprits were caught red handed.

Rewards can be given under M.P. van surksha purskar niyam where you can give upto Rupees 25000/ depending upon value of information.

Though there is budget provisions but it has been observed that even rupees 1000/ was not spend in a year. There is no limitation of budget and I could utilize more than one lakh rupees in a year.

Maintaining informers network and distributing rewards who gave crucial information to prevent crime against wild animal is a must to protect our wild life.

Wild life manager or a director of PA area must follow above practices to protect wild life and catch criminals, to prevent crime and also to make terror in criminals and poachers as to say that you will be caught if you dare to kill any wild animal. In fact whole society will help you in this if you create awareness among society as to why wild life is so important for the very existence of mankind on the earth.

This can be done by writing in news paper about importance of each wild animal, birds etc and telling that hunting of them is an offence punishable under wildlife protection act 1972 for so many years of imprisonment and fine. This will give information to public about the importance of wild life and their duty as a good citizen.

Apart from informers PA managers must keep in touch with territorial staff and officers and local police and must maintain better coordination with them to check poachers. It has been seen that field director, deputy director of a national park do not maintain cordial relationship with their counterpart in charge of territorial forest circle and with district authorities. You are not working in isolation so better and harmonious relations with all above mentioned officers is a must for your success in managing tiger reserve, national park or a sanctuary.

Govt. of India should increase punishment for schedule I and schedule II part II i.e. wild animals which are endangered or about to extinction from 7 years to life imprisonment and minimum punishment should not be less than 7 yrs. Similarly punishment for other wild animals should be maximum 7 yrs and minimum 3 yrs so that people do not try to commit crime on wild animals.

Chapter 11

PROTECTION OF WILD LIFE IN ADJOINING FOREST FROM PA

Tiger reserve has core and buffer area as per amended act of wild life protection act 2006 under 38(V), which under the administration of field director but other PA areas like National park and sanctuary their adjoining forest area are with territorial forest divisions.

Even in case of tiger reserve after buffer adjoining forest is with territorial staff. Tiger is a wanderer animal can travel for more than 400 kilometers and goes to adjoining district or even crosses to another state.

Wild life knows no boundaries and can travel to adjoining forest areas so protection of wild animals in adjoining forest area is utmost important.

These areas should have water holes if not water bodies must be created to sustain them.

In Chapter of habitat improvement various type of water structure has been discussed and they can be built in such a way that at least one water body which must retain water till summer is there to sustain wild life in a radius of 3–5 km.

Even in territorial forest every 3–5 kilometer we must have water body or a small tank, jhiriya or stop dams so that wildlife can remain there. Forest cannot regenerate itself without wildlife so wild life is not just to see but it is important for sustainable forest.

We don't actually give much thought to water availability in the forest or in PA areas whereas it is must for its survival.

So for fanning out population of wild animal's conducive habitat with sufficient water at 3–5 km interval is a must.

In order to sustain and increase wild animal population we must have sufficient water and if it is not there in natural way then we have to create water bodies. Tiger needs lot of water for its survival.

Protection against poachers is more important in these areas because PA areas are mostly protected due to more staff per square kilometer area but territorial forest has less staff and their priority is not wild life but trees. This is the area which is more vulnerable and which needs more protection and habitat which can sustain fanning out population.

Most often poaching is done outside PA areas hence buffer and adjoining areas need more patrolling and protection. Territorial forest staff needs to be educated about importance of wild life and their importance.

Chapter 12

WILD TOURISM AS A TOOL TO CONSERVATION EFFORT

Wild tourism or ecotourism is very popular tourism and it has lot of potential for employment in rural and remote areas. When protected areas are created we stop collection of minor forest produce and all forestry works are to be stopped including felling of trees, regeneration works except road repair and habitat improvement including water management.

It necessitates that those deprived of employment specially tribal of the area must be given equitable employment and tourism is supposed to be an area which gives maximum employment and to all class of people from selling of tea, agricultural produce, milk etc to hotels and to tourists.

Apart from employment wild tourism create awareness to people of India and abroad and specially policy makers to protect forest and wild life for posterity.

High level dignitary visiting an area help to not only make it popular destination but to feel pride of our area having so much pristine forest and wild life as people want to come and see. Local villagers are also motivated to save these wild life areas because of its value as a best tourist destination which they were ignorant till then.

I have seen this in Pench Tiger Reserve Seoni area where till 2001 when I joined there were very low tourism Approximately, 1000 annually due to lack of infrastructure and lack of publicity.

Surrounding villagers do not understand the value of wild animals as a best tourism destination but were angry because they were banned to enter into PA area to collect NWFP (Non wood Forest Produce), which they were collecting since ages and forestry works of timber felling etc has stopped which were supporting their income.

Though National Park was declared in 1983 but since 17 yrs tourism was not catching up. So people did not understand the value of forest and wild life and they were against park and were indulge in illicit grazing inside the park, fire and illicit felling of timber etc.

After it became the popular destination for Indian as well as foreign tourist lot of youth got employment as guide, camp chaukidars, helpers in Hotel and in management of hotels came up to cater the needs of visiting tourist.

VILLAGERS AS STACK HOLDER

Immediately after declaring area as Protected area, adjoining villagers felt deprived as they were using forest for grazing, collecting non wood forest produce and also employed in forestry operations.

It is the duty of Park authority to develop area as tourist destination so that they get employment and value of their land is increased, also their agriculture produce is sold. Villagers become stack holder and help to protect forest area. Hence tourism becomes a tool of conservation.

I have seen villages around Pench tiger reserve like Turiya, Karmajhiri etc. were hostile towards park but after Pench tiger reserve become popular destination they become stack holders and their attitude changed towards park. So many high standard hotels have come up who employ lot of local manpower.

WILD LIFE VALUE IS ESTABLISHED

Tourist coming from all over the world emphasizes the value of that area which was not understood by locals and looking to the flux of tourist around the world they feel excited about their area and value attached to its wild life.

TOURISM BIGGEST EMPLOYER

It is an established fact that tourism industry is the biggest employer of man power. Due to high employment generation people of the area converts as conservationist and this ensures protection of wild life and forest.

Tourism gives employment to all section of society from tea seller to big hotel owners. Agriculture produce like vegetables, flowers, milk, eggs, chicken etc are sold to visitors through hotels and Dhabas. Value of Land is increase to very high rate and this is a giant gain to local villagers to sell some of his /her land and purchase more land away from the place at cheap rates.

People also purchase gypsies for safari to take round to visiting tourist. Overall development of area and economic upliftment of people is a key to the success of wild life protection.

ECONOMICS OF TOURISM

Tourisms contribution in creation of wealth and jobs is universally recognized.

As per WTTC Travel and Tourism Highlight 2016

Foreign Exchange earning Of India from Foreign Tourist - 22.92 billion US $ = 154146 crores rupees

World earning = 22923 US Billion dollar

Total Tourist Arrival (foreign) = 1079696

Total Domestic Tourist to all state = 16136 lakhs

Contribution of Travel and Tourism including direct, indirect and induced impacts to GDP in India was around 6.4% in 2013 WTTC report.

Large number of foreign tourist visits Tiger reserve or national park so it contributes a major part of economy in remote wild areas and lot of jobs is created.

Approximately more than 11 lakh domestic tourists and 92000 foreign tourist visited National parks in M.P. between July 2010 and June 2011 in one year and approx. 60000 jobs were created and rupees 300 crores were spent (Pabla H.S.,2015) Road to nowhere).

People come to national park for adventure, peace, recreation in forest area with nature and delighted to see tiger and other wild animals.

Awareness among children and people visiting Park: - Best use of tiger reserve and other PA areas is to create awareness among children and people regarding importance of wild life. This is the greatest advantage of PA area to create awareness about wild life conservation worldwide.

PA authorities are advised to give concession to local school children to visit park area to see the tiger and other wild animal and they should be properly educated about the importance of each and every animal and birds so that they can become our ambassadors for protection of wild life in PA and other areas. Local public should also be given concession or free trip to visit park as a goodwill mission.

Tiger conservation has improved due to tourism Activity

Tourism in the area keeps our staff vigilant all the time because it is being watched and tourist guides moving along with tourist in vehicle.

It has been seen that PA area which is popular destination has improved tiger and herbivore population. Pench Tiger reserve Seoni M.P. is an example of highest density of prey population and tiger density per square kilometer. This is because habitat improvement and water management helped to increase their population. Protection is improved due to more staff, field camps at strategic points, regular patrolling and active wireless communication.

Change of Focus from timber production to Wild life Management

PA management and wild tourism help to divert timber production towards wild life. This is great advantage of tourism for protection of flora and fauna. Intense working and monitoring by top management gives added advantage for conservation of wild life.

It is not correct that tiger population has declined due to increase in tourism

There are some people who feel that decline in tiger population is due to increase in tourism activity but this is not correct. Panna tiger reserve, Sariska tiger reserve which were not popular tourist destination lost all tigers where as Pench tiger reserve which become a famous destination in 2001 become number one tiger reserve in the country having increased tourism from 1000 tourist to 40000 tourist in 2006 and more than 75000 tourist in 2018 in a small area of 411 square kilometer.

This issue was raised in Honorable Supreme Court in 2013 and new guidelines came up with assumptive factors which were mostly exaggerated which reduced carrying capacity of tourist vehicles to half in order to save tiger.

We allow tourist to only 20% area and disturbance is at most 200 meter in both side but we count area of whole compartment, though actually effective area of disturbance may be only 5%.

Factors responsible for decline in tiger population are lack of water management, protection, poaching in buffer out of fanning out population.

We find that tourism is a tool for conservation and protection of wild life.

Restriction on tourism in tiger reserve by NTCA

After amendment in wild life protection act in 2006 section 38 National Tiger conservation Authority has been came into existence to make guidelines for everything in tiger reserve for making tiger conservation plan to tourism etc and has power to direct state Govt., CWLW and its officer to follow his dictate.

This is welcome step to save tiger and protect habitat from other land use and guide state wild life authorities.

But NTCA has expressed his views before Honorable Supreme court to ban all tourism in PA areas but due to public pressure took u turn to say that it should be permitted to very limited area in core of tiger reserve and should be phased out in due course of time. But it was not accepted and they have issued guidelines as 20% area in core can be used within tourism Zone.

Complete ban on tourism in core area to save tiger is without any scientific study and does not true to the socio economic condition of the area and it is not useful in the conservation and protection of tiger and wild life as well.

Their thinking revolves to declaring critical wild life habitat as per section 2(b) of Forest rights act 2006 where such areas should be kept in violet for the purpose of wild life conservation.

Due to FRA 2006, community rights and personal rights to forest dwelling community can be given even in National park and sanctuaries. state Govt. and MOEF, to save National park and sanctuaries from encroachment or burdening with community rights declared all National park and sanctuary area as critical tiger habitat as inviolate area.

But they are misinterpreting inviolate area to be kept free from tourism but this is not correct for the protection of tiger so also it is against the wildlife protection amendment act 2006 U/S 38(O)(1)(C), which clearly says that NTCA should lay down normative standards for tourism activity and guidelines for project tiger from time to time for tiger conservation in the buffer and core area of tiger reserve and ensure their due compliance.

Due to new guidelines carrying capacity has reduced to 50% which will be discussed in the next Chapter.

But it has proved beyond doubt that increase in tiger population is higher in tourism Zone than in other core zone not open to tourist, also poaching is not reported in tourism zone though it has happened in other area of tiger reserve.

This is because of round the time surveillance by staff due to presence of tourist and also by tourist guide. Any mismanagement or slackness by staff is reported by tourist so the staff posted in tourism zone is on the toes and always alert.

With regulated tourism it does not disturb tiger or any wildlife as they do not recognize and do not bothered with our presence unless we disturb them by chasing or going very close to them. Tiger is the king of the jungle and he is not bothered to human presence. So too much conservative approach is a wild opinion and it is not good for wild life protection itself.

We are democratic country and opinion of majority matters and think of situation where NTCA wanted to ban all tourism activity in PA then none would be able to appreciate what is there in PA. Visiting National parks by VIPs for sighting of wild animals spreads awareness in public which also follow them which helps promoting tourism and wild life conservation.

We know that visit by our Prime minister Indira Gandhi and Rajeev Gandhi to Kanha National park has created awareness and thought to must visit National park as to see what special feeling is there. Unless people are allowed to visit core areas of PA we cannot protect it and we cannot muster support of policy makers for conserving our wild life.

Due to shrinking of land resources people are encroaching forest land and they say that whether tiger is important or human being is important.

In this scenario we should be realistic and I feel that if you take 20% core area of tiger reserve for tourism then 100 meter both side will be taken as disturbance area and that should be calculated for counting as areas open for tourism which should be 20% area of the PA. In order to count 20% area new roads may be open for tourism. At present whole compartment area is counted which is in the tourist road but it would have been counted only 100 meter on both sides.

ECONOMIC SUSTENANCE

As per Pabla H.S. 2015, in the year 2011–12, there were 102 national parks and 515 sanctuaries in the country the annual allocation by MOEF and CC was only 56.52 core rupees where as NTCA gave away 145 crores rupees and after distributing it on and average it comes to just 32.60 lakh rupees which is minuscule amount. MP got Approximately Rupees 46 crores and our own revenue collection was rupees 20 crores.

Bulk of the NTCA money was for relocation of villages, so it is very obvious that National Park and sanctuaries are benefited and maintained due to gate money collected from National parks and which is utilized for the welfare of National park and surrounding villages. This money is also used for such works for which there is no budget.

State Govt. gives salaries and other Tour expenses to its employees but Central Govt. should allocate more recourse to save these pristine habitat and wild life for the very existence of mankind.

PA areas are the source of water to river and they conserve and release water to make rivers perennial. Their main contribution apart from wild life conservation is huge source of water to the river. Protected Areas are the reservoir of biodiversity and gene pool of many plants, animal, birds and micro organism for use in posterity.

PA is our show room to show to public as what can be if forest is protected and how much biodiversity it can have.

This is the source of fresh unpolluted air and people will love to spend few days to feel good health in pristine forest.

So we can very well say that tourism is very well an effective tool for conservation of wild life in Tiger reserve, National parks and sanctuaries.

We should try to develop more PA area as tourist destination by habitat improvement of that area, publicity and tourist facility.

In M.P. though we have 9 National parks and 25 sanctuaries but tourism is mostly in Kanha, Bandhavgarh, Pench and Panna. Van vihar national park and zoo is visited due to its location in the heart of the city Bhopal. But Sanjay National Park Sidhi is yet to attract tourist.

All sanctuaries and National park has its own beauty and variety and if properly managed with some creative work, habitat improvement and tourism facilities are developed then it will reduce the burden of busy Tiger reserves and also create awareness to local population for conservation and will also generate local employment in remote area.

Karmajhiri Forest Rest House: Photo by R. G. Soni

Tiger Sighting in Safari: Photo by Pranay Soni

Tiger Sighting on Elephant Back: Photo by Pranay Soni

Tourists Waiting For Elephant Ride: Photo by Pranay Soni

Mowgli hut outer sitting in Night: Photo by Pranay Soni

Chapter 13

CARRYING CAPACITY OF PA FOR TOURIST VEHICLES AND ITS IMPACT ON REDUCTION OF TOURISTS

In order to limit tourists NTCA has given a guideline for carrying capacity of vehicles in Tiger reserve to Honorable Supreme Court in the year 2013 which is binding on Authorities of PA.

Formula is assumptive and presumptive and made of imaginary factors without any scientific basis or research which resulted in 50% reduction of tourists in all tiger reserves as compared to last year tourist numbers.

NTCA has predetermined to reduce tourist to just half without any substantial reasoning which resulted in loss of jobs and employment of rural people.

Field Directors of M.P. national park and tiger reserve did not put up factors properly which resulted in 50% reduction of per day vehicle numbers where as Maharashtra state has given factors and data in such a way that its carrying capacity kept as it is.

M.P. Wild life Wing tried to say that it is the Honorable Supreme courts direction to follow these guidelines but the fact is not as told by forest Deptt., but the fact is that M.P. has given factors which are not correct but given in such a way so that carrying capacity is reduced drastically.

Factors was given by M.P. himself and if there is any change of local factors it can be changed by Local area committee headed by commissioner and where field directors and some representatives of hotel and lodges etc are the members.

CONCERN DUE TO REDUCTION IN CARRYING CAPACITY OF VEHICLES

It has reduced tourist influx to 50% and due to this reduction many hotel and lodges became uneconomical to run and they have to close its establishment. Lot of guide lost jobs and employment has reduced accordingly.

NTCA assumption of no tourist or very less tourist in core area to save wild life is not based on scientific research because tiger and other wild animal population has increased in tourism zone as compared to non tourism zone due to better habitat, more protection and round the day surveillance.

NTCA GUIDELINES FOR CARRYING CAPACITY OF VEHICLES

Mistakes in calculating various Factors:-

Mistakes in applying Guidelines of NTCA in Pench Tiger Reserve M.P.

Estimation of visitor carrying capacity as per revised guidelines submitted by NTCA to Honorable Supreme court for tourism in and around tiger reserve:

Pench Tiger Reserve Seoni M.P.
Core Area - 411.330 sqkm
Tourism Area - 84.760 sqkm
(Made 20% after supreme court judgment dated 16.10.2012, previously it was 150 sq km)
Road Length - 116 km (previously it was 145 km)

Note: - 20% area in tourism zone was calculated in such a way that whole compartment area was counted if road passes through it where as only you should take disturbance area 100 meter both side in total length of the road.

By this way we are using only 23.2 Sq km area of park which is just 5.6% where as you can use 84 sq km area and you can increase tourism zone to make it 20%.

So there is scope in increasing more road length. NTCA has said to take whole compartment area whereas it should not be more than 100 meter both side of road. Earlier NTCA prescribed 100 meter both side then change to whole compartment passing through the road, this is ridiculous.

(a) Physical carrying capacity (PCC)

This is the maximum number of vehicles that can physically fit into a space, over a particular time. It is expressed as following -

$$PCC = AxV/axRf$$

where A = available area for public use

v/a = one visitor /sq meter

Rf = rotation factor (number of visit per day)

In order to measure PCC, The following criteria must be taken into account;. Only vehicular movement on forest roads are permitted hence road length is more relevant than area.

➤ Standing area is not relevant but closeness between vehicles is important.

➤ There is a required distance of at least 500 meter (1/2km) between two vehicles to avoid dust (2 vehicles /km)

➤ At least 3 hrs are needed for a single park excursion.

➤ The PA is open to tourist for 9 months in a year and almost 9 hrs per day.

➤ Linear road length (for tourist)=116 km

Rotation factor = opening period /average time of one visit =9/3=3

Physical Carrying capacity (PCC) = 116 kmX2 vehicles /km x3= 696 visits/day

(b) Real carrying capacity (RCC)
RCC is the maximum permissible number of visits to a site, once the reductive factors (corrective) derived from the particular characteristics of biophysical, environmental, ecological, and social and management variables.

RCC= PCC x Cf1 x Cf2 x ——-Cfn

Where Cf is a corrective factor expressed as a percentage. Thus the formula for calculating RCC is

RCC= PCC x 100-cf1/100 x 100-cf2/100 x
——100-cfn/100

Corrective Factors are site specific and are expressed in percentage as below:

Cf= M1X100/Mt

Where Cf = corrective factor, M1 =limiting magnitude of the variables

Mt = total magnitude of the variables

(i) **Road erosion: here the susceptibility of the site is taken into account.**
Total road length= 116 km
Medium erosion sink= 20km (weighing factor=2)
High erosion risk = 10km (weighing factor =3)

$$M1= 20x2+10x3=70km$$

$$Mt =116 \ km$$

$$Cf1 = \frac{70km}{116km} \ x100= 60\%$$

This assumption is totally baseless as roads in tourism zone are not affected due to erosion hence taking 60% road length for erosion factor is baseless and it can maximum be taken as 20%. **So cf1 = 20%,**

So, Cf1 should have been taken 20% and not 60%

(ii) Disturbance to wild life:

Here, species which are prone to disturbance owing to tourist visits are considered. The peak courtship activity for spotted deer last for two months before the onset of regular monsoon. As for as tigers are concerned, newborns are seen between March and May and also during rains, hence an average value of two months in a year can be considered as the matter of fact. And 9 months are total tourist visiting month in a year hence

Correction Factor (CF)

Corrective Factor for Spotted deer (2months)

$$Cfw1 = 2/9 \ x100= 22.2\%$$

Corrective factor for Tiger (2months)

$$Cfw2 = 2/9 \ x100= 22.2\%$$

Overall corrective factor for disturbance of wild life in India in Pench Tiger Reserve

$$Cfw= Cfw1+cfw2= 22.2+22.2=44.4\% \ or \ 44\%$$

(iii) Temporary closing of Roads:

For maintenance or other managerial reasons, visits, to certain roads may be temporarily restricted within the protected area. The corrective factor in this regard is calculated as

$$Cft = \frac{\text{Limiting weeks/year x 100}}{\text{Total weeks/year}}$$

In pench, an average value of 2 limiting weeks per year may be considered as the limiting weeks, and thus the corrective factor works out to:

$$Cft = \frac{\text{2 weeks /year x 100}}{\text{36 week /year}} = 5.5\% \text{ or } 6\%$$

At present there is half day closure on Wednesday. Due to this, temporary closing of roads has been reduced to 2 weeks per year from 5 weeks per year as considered in the earlier working.

Computation of RCC

RCC = PCCx 100-cfe/100 x100-cfw/100 x 100-cft/100

RCC = 696 x100–60/100 x100–44/100 x100–6/100

= 696 x.40x.56 x.94

= 146 or 147 visits per day

(C) Effective permissible carrying capacity (EPCC):
The EPCC is the maximum number of visitors that a site can sustain, given the management capacity (MC) available. EPCC is obtained by multiplying the real carrying capacity (RCC) with the management capacity. MC is defined as the sum of conditions that PA administration requires if it is to carry out its functions at the optimum level. Limitation in management like lack of staff and infrastructure limit the RCC.

For Pench, owing to the paucity of staff the MC is around 60%

Managerial capacity = 60%

Hence EPCC = RCCxMC = 147x 0.60= 88.2 say 88 vehicles /day

Thus the effective permissible carrying capacity on any week day is only 88 vehicles per day.

Managerial capacity has been wrongly calculated as there needs to be staff in only three gets and every vehicle is with tourist guide, moreover Deptt. Should also calculate the number of daily wagers employed as camp chaukidars in the strength of staff.

If we take it as 80%

Then EPCC= 147 x0.80 =117 vehicles per day

And if MC is taken as 100%

Then EPCC = 147 vehicles per day

Assumptive Error:-

It has been seen that wrong assumption has been taken

1. Road erosion: it is exaggerated and it should be only 20%

2. Managerial Capacity; - it should have been taken as 80%

3. Calculation of Tourism Zone area 20%:-

It should be calculated by multiplying 100 meter both side of road to the road length so that it is 20% of PA area.

Here it is 200 meter x116000mt =2320 hectare

I.e. 23.20 sq km which is only 5.6% area is open to tourism whereas it can be 20% of the area of PA, hence more area can be taken in tourism zone and more road length could be added for tourist zone.

In M.P. while calculating carrying capacity it seems that it has been predetermined to reduce carrying capacity to just half, but in Maharashtra adjoining Pench M.P. factors were calculated in such a way as its carrying capacity was intact to previous level.

If we calculate the carrying capacity of Pench Tiger Reserve M.P. as stated above by only changing the erosion factor as 20% in place of 60% which is factually correct and all other factor as it is then it will be -

RCC = 696x 100–20/100x.56x.94 =293 vehicle per day

EPCC = 293 x 0.60 = 175 vehicles per day

Which will be correct and it needs to be revised at 175 vehicles per day from just 88 vehicles and this will double the tourist and will not do any harm to the park and it is based on the formula suggested in NTCA guidelines.

Similarly carrying capacity of all tiger reserve and national park needs revision on the basis of prevailing factors as per NTCA guidelines and i am sure if factors are properly calculated then carrying capacity of each PA will be doubled.

Comparison of Maharashtra and M.P. National park Carrying capacity prior to October 2012 and after:

S.N	Name of TR	Area	Road length	No of V	After V.
1	BandhavgarhTr	716 sqkm	246km	130	88
2	Kanha TR	917 sqkm	240km	292	140
3	Pench TR M.P.	411 sqkm	116 km	130	88
4	Panna TR	576 sqkm		140	70
5	Satpura Tr	1339 sqkm		24	24
6	Tadoba Tr MS	625 sqkm		117	112
7	Pench MS	257 sqkm	179 km	100	100

This Data clearly shows that in M.P. carrying capacity has been reduced to half which needs to be revised. Local area committee headed by Commissioner with field directors as members can reassess the factors prevailing there and recommend it to PCCF wild life who can revise carrying capacity.

This is totally wrong assumption that due to tourism tiger population has declined or it has bad effect on wild life, on the contrary wild life population has increased in tourism zone.

Due to drastic reduction of carrying capacity In M.P. employment in remote area has been drastically reduced around PA which will create man animal conflict.

Proper and just tourism which is properly regulated will help Wild life and local population in their development.

Chapter 14

THE TRUE STORY OF MOWGLI AND THE AREA OF "THE JUNGLE BOOK"

Case study:

**Success story of Pench Tiger Reserve the best
Tiger Reserve of INDIA
Mowgli: A character in the friction Novel
*"The Jungle Book"***

Pench Tiger Reserve Seoni (M.P.) is the real land of Mowgli, and The Area of famous **"The Jungle Book"**.

Rudyard Kipling was awarded the Noble prize of Literature in 1907 for his brilliant literary work in literature which includes "The Jungle book".

There existed a real human child who was nurtured by wolves. This child was caught by Lieut. John Moor under the Guidance of Col. William Sleeman in the year 1831 near Seoni. Rudyard Kipling took the clue from The book "Rambles and Recollection " written by Col. William Sleeman Title " wolf nurturing children " and from a semi autobiographical Novel written by R.A. Strandel, " Seonee Camp Life in Satpuda hills ".

SEARCH OF UNIQUE SELLING POINT (USP)

For Pench Tiger reserve search for USP ended in discovery of Mowgli and the Jungle book Area

I joined as Field Director Pench Tiger reserve Seoni on 9 th June 2001. Main Task given to me by The Late shri Harbans sing the then Forest Minister of M.P. who belongs to Seoni district was to bring this National Park in a position that at least people from M.P. new that there is a National park in Seoni District.

At that time Kanha Tiger reserve and Bandhavgarh Tiger reserve were two famous wild tourism destinations in M.P. Though Pench tiger reserve Seoni Was declared a National Park in the year 1983 and it was a sanctuary since 1977 but it was not popular as tourist destination. Annual visitors were Approximately 1000 and there were no private hotel to stay, and only one old Forest Rest House built in 1920 at Karmajhiri was there with 6 extra cottages constructed by District fund.

My main task was to make this place popular for tourists apart from wild life management.

I posed a question to me as to **why any person should visit Pench Tiger reserve?**, When World famous Kanha Tiger reserve is nearby.

If this question is answered then only we can make this area popular for tourists.

You need an USP (unique selling point) to make any place a popular destination. This resulted into search for an USP to promote this area for Tourism.

Tourism and conservation of wild life goes hand by Hand, unless an area is a popular destination nobody in Govt. will look into its development and area will remain as it is as was the case with this place since 1983 when it was made national park and in 1992 it was declared a tiger reserve, since 17 years it was not in a priority and it was not a famous destination with poor accommodation, so how people will come?.

Wild life Manager has to look into the aspect of tourism promotion as it helps to bring to lime light and in the knowledge of Govt. and due to tourism you create jobs in the area and local people becomes stack holders of the Park.

If any P.A. (Protected Area) area is not popular it will be neglected and we will lose wild life as well.

DISCOVERY OF THE JUNGLE BOOK AREA AND MOWGLI

It was a chance discovery while I was passing through Nainpur a town in the border of Seoni District coming from Kanha Tiger Reserve by Road that i could recollect that it was told when i was probationer in South Seoni Division in the year 1984 by Then Deputy Director Pench National Park Mr. Amar sing Parihar that Mowgli was there between Nainpur and Kanha area (Mandla District).

Nainpur was just in the border of Seoni District that i told to range officer Mr. Dondway accompanying with me that we can definitely claim that Mowgli is from our district i.e. Seoni, my Range officer Told me that Story of Mowgli is from Seoni District as told by one reporter of a news paper. I told him to bring him to my Office today.

Discussion with reporter I was told by him that Mr. Kailash Narad Retd., History Professor from Jabalpur has done research in Sir William Henry Sleeman and his work.

I went to meet Kailash Narad in Jabalpur the next day and he has shown me the article published in a Hindi Magazine

"Dharmyug" which is Hindi version of article published in the novel "The Rambles and Recollection by Col. William Sleeman in the year 1831, which contains the drawing of Wolf boy in that time and the story is of Wolf nurturing Child in Seoni district which was named Mowgli in frictional Novel "The Jungle Book".

एक था

मोगली

This boy, named Mowgli, brought up by a herd of wolves was found in the Sant Bawadi village by Leul. John Moor under the guidance of Col. William Sleeman in 1831. Kipling got this flamboyant description of things both from the pamphlet titled, "An account of wolves nurturing children in their dens" by Sir. William Henry Sleeman and a book on 'Camp Life of Seoni" by R.A. Sterendale. The Jungle Book mentions a place where Sher Khan was killed. This place is in fact the Valley of Benganga River, near Kanhiwada village. At the present time, these places of historical significance are falling under the famous Pench National Park.

Sketch of a boy caught in the Jungle's of Seoni in the Year 1831 by Lt. John Moor.

" This boy, named Mowgli, brought up by a herd of wolves was found in the Sant Bawadi

Mowgli was caught in the year 1831 in the village Chor Bavdi, 74 miles away from Jabalpur. I have seen the 74 Mile stone which is approximately 10 km from Seoni towards Jabalpur.

Then I readout the jungle Book in which the first page, there is a mention of Seonee hills and wolf pack, Present day Seoni district was written as Seonee in Brithish Days.

Vain Ganga River originates from the jungle of Pench Tiger Reserve. There is mention of Pench River which passes from inside the Pench Tiger Reserve which cuts the Park into two equal Half.

Name of places and stories were taken from the Semi Auto biographical Novel" Seonee; camp life in Satpuda hills" by R.A. Strandel.

In this Novel there is a mention of a notorious Tiger, operating between Kurai and Rukhad in the heart of Pench tiger reserve Seoni (M.P.), which killed approximately 150 people but not hunted down by any Hunter at that time.

The Tiger when he was old and could not kill wild animal started killing cattle and humans and was operating nearer to Seoni, this tiger was given the name of Sher khan The villain in the Novel.

Village Kanhiwada, Amodagarh are all mentioned in the Jungle book. Sidhaghat the place where Vain Ganga makes vertical fall is the place described in the Jungle book as the place where Mowgli Killed the Sherkhan in Seoni District.

So it was established that the boy who was captured during Col. Sleeman time in the company of wolves was given the name of Mowgli and the forest of Seoni, Pench Tiger Reserve is the area of the jungle Book.

मोगली के पकड़े जाने की सच्ची कहानी

धर्मयुग 27 जून 1982 * हिन्दी भाषा मे * विलियम स्लीमन
द्वारा लंदन मे प्रकाशित
रोमांचक
संत बावड़ी का वह
मानवभक्षी नरभेड़िया
* कैलाश नारद

रोमांचक

संत बावड़ी का यह मानवभक्षी नरभेड़िया कैलाश नारद

साखू का यह विशाल जंगल सतपुड़ा के पठार से उतरता हुआ पुरे दक्षिण की उपत्यकाओं तक चला गया था, गहन और अगम्य, उस जंगल की छत अब भी जब-तब नजर आ जाती है, लेकिन छितरी हुई, बीच में जबलपुर-नागपुर रोड़ चला गया है, यह गांव अब भी है, लेकिन बसे यहां रूकती नहीं, गांव का नाम है, संत बावड़ी, छोटी-छोटी झोपड़ पट्टियों और नमी तथा महुए के दरक्तों के बीच ऊंघता हुआ-सा, लेकिन साढ़े पांच सौ घरों की इस छोटी सी बस्ती में ईस्ट इंडिया कंपनी के जमाने में अपने यहां घट रही अजीबो गरीब और असामान्य सी वारदातों के कारण समूचे सागर-नर्मदा भू-भाग को उद्वेलित कर दिया था और तो और, ठगी-दमन के अप्रतिम महानायक विलियम स्लीमैन भी संत बावड़ी की घटनाओं से बैचेन हो उठे थे और सन 1831 में खुद घोड़े पर सवार हो कर, चौरासी मील (135 कि.मी.) का सफर तय करते हुए संत बावड़ी आ पहुंचे थे, ताकि मौके पर मौजूद रह कर वे खुद उन पैशाचिक सी प्रतीत होने वाली घटनाओं का अध्ययन कर सकें, लेकिन, तीन दिन, तीन रात रूक कर भी संत बावड़ी में जब कुछ हासिल नहीं हुआ था विलियम स्लीमैन को, तो अपने मातहत लेपिटनेंट जॉन मूर को संत बावड़ी में छोड़कर वे वापस जबलपुर लौट गये थे। जॉन मूर को उन्होंने जाते-जाते, हिदायतें दे दी थीं, यदि किसी भी प्रकार के रहस्य का उद्घाटन होता है, तो वे तत्काल उसकी सूचना उन्हें दें।

ऐसा क्या हो रहा था संत बावड़ी में?

उन्नीसवीं सदी का यह अंधकाराच्छन्न भारत रबत-बीज जैसे उग आये इतिहास के क्रूरतम हत्यारों, ठगों, के नृशंश कारनामों से भर गया था। पीले रुमाल के फंदे से अपने शिकार का गला घोंट देनेवाले उन अराजक हत्यारों के हाथों में खून के तजुर्बे थे और आंखों में भी रक्त की प्यास। ईस्ट इंडिया कंपनी की हुकूमत का यह सबसे कलंकित इतिहास था, जब गंगा-जमुना के दोआबो से लेकर नर्मदा-कावेरी के कछार तक गुमनाम और बेशिनाख्त लाशों से भरते जा रहे थे। विलियम स्लीमैन पहले फिरंगी अफसर थे, जिन्होंने ठगों की क्रूरताओं के खिलाफ सर्वाधिक प्रचंड स्वर मुखर किया था। उन्हीं के प्रयासों का फल था कि भारत तत्कालीन गवर्नर जनरल लॉर्ड विलियम बेंटिक ने उन्हीं विलियम स्लीमैन के नेतृत्व में ठगी उन्मूलन विभाग कायम किया था और विभाग का मुख्यालय रखा था जबलपुर। स्लीमैन के जो विश्ववस्त साथी सागर-नर्मदा भू-भाग में तैनात थे, उन्हीं में से एक थे जॉन मूर। ये सिवनी बालाघाट जिलों के प्रभारी थे और ठगों का दमन कर रहे थे। नागपुर से जबलपुर जानेवाली सड़क पर स्थित यह गांव संत बावड़ी ठगों की आखेट भूमि माना जाता था और इतना बदनाम हो गया था कि लोगों ने उसे ठग- वाबड़ी कहना शुरू कर दिया था । पिछले कुछ दिनों में, डेढ़ माह में उस गांव के बत्तीस व्यक्ति गायब हो चुके थे और खयाल किया था कि बदनाम ठगों ने ही उन अभागों को लूटने क बाद मार डाला था और उनकी लाश गायब कर दी थी।

लेफ्टिनेंड जॉन मूर ने तहकीकात शुरू की, लेकिन गुत्थियां इतनी थी कि वह उलझ कर रह गया। गायब हुए व्यक्ति न तो मालदार आसामी थे और न ही दूर-दराज की यात्रा पर जाने-वाले धर्माभिलाषी तीर्थयात्री, जो कि आमतौर पर ठगों का शिकार बनते थे। इसके ठीक विपरीत, लापता हुए अधिकांश अभागों में औरतों और बच्चों की तादाद ज्यादा थी और इसी बिन्दु पर जॉन मूर की अक्ल चकरा गयी थी। औरतों और बच्चों का वध ठगों की आचरण संहिता में वर्जित था और जो तीन व्यक्ति, इनके अलावा, लापता थे। उनमें एक था गांव के दुधारू पशु चरानेवाला गडरिया और दो थे पखावज तथा सितार बजानेवाले, जो छपारा के एक विवाह समारोह से संत बावड़ी वापस आते समय एका-एक लुप्त हो गये थे। ठगों

की आचरण संहिता में गडरिया और संगीतकार भी हत्या के लिए निषिद्ध थे। इन बत्तीस अभागों की हत्या यदि ठगों ने नहीं की थी, तब किसने उन्हें गायब किया था और किस उद्देश्य से अपहरण किया गया था उनका?

गुत्थियां उलझती ही गयी

जॉन मूर का शक सबसे पहले आसपास की पहाड़ियों में रहनेवाले भीलों पर गया। लेकिन खुद उनके बीच की कई औरतें और बच्चे लापता हो चुके थे और उनमें भयावह आतंक व्याप्त था। वे इस बुरी तरह से डरे हुए थे कि उन्हें लगने लगा था कि कोई पैशाचिक शक्ति इस तरह के शैतानियत भरे काम कर रही है। ऐसी आधिभौतिक शक्तियों के शमन हेतु लापता व्यक्तियों के रिश्तेदारों में बस्ती के ओझा के कहने पर मुर्गे ओर बकरे की बलि भी चढ़ाई थी, लेकिन उत्पात तब भी रूका नहीं था।

मुमकिन है, इस उत्पात के पीछे कोई बाघ हो, जॉन मूर को लगा, लेकिन उसका यह शक भी बेबुनियाद साबित हुआ, क्योंकि उस इलाके में न तो किसी बाघ के पहले से होने की कोई जानकारी थी और ना ही कही किसी बाघ के पंजे का निशान नजर आया था।

तब, जॉन मूर का ध्यान गया लकड़बग्घों और भेड़ियों की तरफ। लोग जिस तरीके से गायब हो रहे थे, यह भेड़ियों का ही कारनामा प्रतीत हो रहा था। जो अभागे लापता हो रहे थे, उन्हे रात के तीसरे पहर बरामदों में से उठाया गया था और उनकी हड़िडयां भी नहीं मिली थी. जंहा शेर और बाघ अपने शिकार की हड़िडयाँ छोंड देते हैं वंहा लकद्बग्घे और भेड़िये हड़िडयां तक हजम कर जाते हैं । वे हड़िडयाँ चबाने के खास शौकीन होते है, लेकिन संत बावड़ी के गुमशुदा व्यक्तियों की लकड़बग्घों और भेड़ियो ने ही मारा था, इसका भी कोई प्रमाण नहीं था, क्योंकि समूचे इलाके में भेड़िये या उस जैसे किसी पशु के पैर का निशान भी जॉन मूर को नहीं मिला। कुछ अजीबोगरीब निशान जरूर लापता व्यक्तियों के घरों के इर्द-गिर्द मिले थे, जिन्होंने ईस्ट इंडिया कंपनी के सिपाहियों को उलझने और भी ज्यादा बढ़ी दी। वे निशान पंजों के चिन्ह जरूर थे, मगर किस पशु के? वे चार गोल-गोल और कांफी गहरे निशान थे, जिनके पीछे कुछ ऐसे चिन्ह थे, मानो चौड़े ब्रश से बनाये गये हो। फरलांग, दो फरलांग तक तो वे काफी साफ नजर आते फिर एकाएक गायब

हो जाते ऐसी जगह पर, जहां न तो कोई झुरमुट होता और ना ही जंगल और ना ही नदी या पहाड़। धुर मैदान पर पहुंच कर सपाट जमीन पर विलीन हुए मिलते, वे अजीबोगरीब निशान।

नरभेड़िया: लेफ्टिनेंड जॉन मूर द्वारा बनाये गये स्केच की विष्णु अग्निहोत्री निर्मित अनुकृति

ऐसे निशान और उनकी अनिश्चित स्थिति ने समूचे संत बावड़ी गांव को बौखला दिया था। ग्रामीण जन मानने लगे थे कि जो लोग गायब हो रहे है वे किसी प्रेतात्मा का शिकार बन रहे है और वे विचित्र से निशान जरूर उसी पिशाच के उल्टे पैरों के हैं, जो रात के अंधेरो में आ कर चुपके से अपने शिकार को उठाकर ले जाता है।

फिर, एक रात एक ग्रामवासी की झोपड़ी से एक बच्चा गायब हुआ। वह अपनी मां के साथ सो रहा था। आधी रात के लगभग, मां ने अपने इर्द-गिर्द कुछ सरसराहट सी जरूर सुनी थी और जब तक वह उठ कर बैठ सके, बच्चा गायब था। यह वारदात झोंपडी के भीतर हुई थी। लेकिन दरवाजा खुला था। सशंकित मां यह सोच कर बाहर आयी कि मुमकिन है बच्चा बाहर लुढक गया हो, लेकिन बच्चा बाहर भी नहीं था।

भौचक्की-सी वह औरत पागलों जैसी अपने बच्चे की तलाश में यहां वहां दौड़ने लगी। शोर सुन कर दूसरे लोग बाहर निकल आये। झोंपडी के बाहर किसी पशु के पदचिन्ह नहीं थे। लेकिन खून जरूर छितरा हुआ था। जाहिर था कि बच्चे की हत्या हो चुकी थी।

खबरदार! उसे जिंदा ही पकड़ना है

लेकिन हत्यारा कौन था?

जॉन मूर ने शिकारी कुत्तों, सिपाहियों और गांव वालों को ले कर, उसी रात संत बावड़ी और उसके आसपास मीलों दूर का इलाका छान मारा, लेकिन खूनी का कोई निशान उन्हें नहीं मिला। झोंपड़ी के आस-पास ये ही रहस्यमय चिन्ह जरूर मिले जॉन मूर को, वही चार गोल, गहरे निशान - दो आगे, दो पीछे, कोई 40 से.मी. के अंतर पर, पिछले निशान अगले चिन्हों के मुकाबले अपेक्षाकृत बड़े थे। अगले निशानों से जुड़े हुए थे वे ब्रश जैसी किसी अबूझ वस्तु से बने हुए चिन्ह, जिनके पीछे-पीछे धूल की लकीर सी चली गयी थी। थोड़े फासले पर जा कर वे पैशाचिक से निशान गायब हो गये थे।

गांव में छाया आतंक इस घटना से और ज्यादा बढ़ गया और फिर दो दिन बाद जब एक सुनार भी अपने घर से इसी तरह गायब हो गया, तब तो समूचा माहौल जैसे हिल उठा, लेफ्टिनेंट जॉन मूर की परेशानी इस वारदात से ओर ज्यादा बढ़ गयी। वह समझ नहीं पा रहा था कि इस अज्ञात और रहस्यमय हत्यारे का मुकाबला वह कैसे करे।

दोपहर को जब वह अपने बंगले के बरामदे में बैठा था, एक बूढ़ा दाखिल हुआ। जॉन मूर उसे पहचान गया। वह संत बावड़ी की ग्राम पंचायत का सरपंच भीकन साव था। वह अपने साथ एक बेहद सनसनीखेज सूचना लेकर आया था।

"पिछली रात मैंने उस राक्षस को अपनी आंखों से देखा, साहब," भीकन साव ने कहा "वह पहले आदमी जैसा था। फिर वह कुत्ते जैसा बन गया और देखते ही देखते गायब हो गया।

जॉन मूर के साथ बैठे ईस्ट इंडिया कंपनी के दूसरे अफसर भीकन साव की बात सुन कर हंसने लगे, लेकिन जॉन मूर संजीदा रहा आया। उसे न जाने क्यों ऐसा महसूस हुआ था कि सरपंच के कथन में सच्चाई थी। उसने अपने अर्दली अब्दुल रहमान को अपने पास बुलाया और उसे जमीन पर घुटनों और कोहनियों के बल चलने के लिए कहा। अब्दुल रहमान उसी मुद्रा में जमीन पर चला, और इस तरह चलने से जो निशान धूल पर बने, वे बहुत कुछ उन रहस्यमय चिन्हों जैसे ही थे। जॉन मूर की आंखें चमक उठी।

'ऐसे ही निशान गांव से बाहर जंगल में बने शिव मंदिर के भी पास मैंने अपनी आंखों से देखे है, साहब' भीकन साव ने जॉन मूर से कहा।

संत बावड़ी से लगभग दो कि.मी. दूर, घनघोर जंगल में एक पहाड़ी नाले के किनारे सदियों पुराना एक शिव मंदिर बना हुआ था। उसका शिखर और बुर्ज टूट गये थे, सिर्फ खंडहर बचा रह गया था। दिन की रोशनी में भी वह बीहड़ बेहद भयावना प्रतीत होता था। लोग वहां से निकलने में कतराते थे।

जॉन मूर के साथ आये सिपाहियों ने शिवमंदिर के इर्द-गिर्द घेरा डाल दिया। वहां की जमीन दलदली थी और उस पर वे रहस्यमय चिन्ह बखूबी नजर आ रहे थे। उनके साथ-साथ एक भेड़िये के पैरों के निशान भी गीली जमीन पर अंकित थे। शिवमंदिर के आस-पास

गहरा सन्नाटा था। जब हवा चलती, तो वहां उगी घास और झुरमुटों में सरसराहट होती, फिर सब खामोश हो जाता। सिपाहियों ने उन झुरमुटों में पत्थर फेंके, लेकिन वहां कोई हल-चल नहीं हुई, जॉन मूर मंदिर के प्रवेश द्वार की तरफ बढा।

गर्भगृह सूना था। वहां सिर्फ टूटा हुआ शिवलिंग और खंडित वेदी मौजूदथी और था गहरा अंधेरा। मशाल जलाकर वहां रोशनी की गयी। लेकिन भीतर कोई भी नजर नहीं आया। जॉन मूर और सिपाही बाहर निकल आये। तभी मंदिर की उत्तरी दीवार के पास एक पत्थर पर लहू की ताजी बूंदें और मानव केशों का एक गुच्छा एक सिपाही को दिखाई दिया। वहां, ऊपर मंदिर की मेहराब ढह गई थी और उसकी दीवार कुछ ऐसी गिरी थी कि वहां एक गुफा सी बन गयी थी। दीवार पर भी लहू के कुछ छींटे गांववालों की नजर आये।

पत्थरों पर चढ कर कुछ लोग टूटी हुई मेहराब के पास पहुंचे। उन्होंने उस गुफा में जैसे ही झांकना चाहा, भीतर से निकल कर कोई बडी तेजी से उन पर झपटा।

वह एक भेडिया था। बुरी तरह से गुर्रा रहा था वह। इसके पहले कि वह किसी को क्षति पहुंचाता, जॉन मूर की पिस्तौल से गोली निकली और मृत भेडिया जमीनपर आ गिरा। लेफ्टिनेंट जॉन मूर ने देखा, उसके मूंह में खून लगा हुआ था। गुफा में सुनार की अधखायी लाश पडी थी। उसका पेट फाड डाला गया था और बांह कंधे से टूट कर झूल रही थी लेकिन उसकी बांह पर किसी आदमी के दांतों के चिन्ह मौजूद थे।

कौन था वह नरराक्षस? क्या सचमुच वहीं, जिसे सरपंच भीकन साव ने अपनी आंखों से देखा था? लेकिन भेडिये की उस अंधियारी, भयानक गुफा में वह क्या करने आया था?

मंदिर के पिछवाडे उगे घने झुरमुट पहाडी नाले तक चले गये थे। जॉन मूर के साथ आये सिपाहियों ने बडी तेजी से उन झुरमुटों में पत्थर फेंकने शुरू कर दिये।

इस सामूहिक अभियान का अनुकूल परिणाम नजर आया। जल्दी ही घनी झाडियों में दुबका हुआ वह नर राक्षस उन्हें मिल गया। सिपाहियों और गांववालों ने उसे घेर लिया और बरछे तान कर वे उसकी ओर बढने लगे, तभी जॉन मूर चिल्लिया, "खबरदार, उसे जिंदा ही पकडना है,"

वह एक नर भेडिया था प्रकृति की ऐसी अनूठी कृति, जिसे जॉन मूर पहली दफा देख रहा था। ईस्ट इंडिया कंपनी के उस बितानी अफसर के लिए वह एक अनोखा अनुभव था।

अपने को घिरा हुआ पा कर उस नरभेडिये ने भाग निकलने की कोशिश की। जब सिपाही उसके काफी करीब पहुंच गये, तो उनमें से दो सिपाहियों पर वह नर भेडिया पूरी शक्ति के साथ टूट पडा और अपने बुरी तरह से बढे हुए नाखूनों से उसने उनके चेहरों को नोच लिया और तीसरे सिपाही के कंधे पर इस बुरी तरह से दांत गडाये कि वहां से गोश्त का एक टुकडा ही कट कर अलग हो गया।

सिपाहियों और गांववालों ने उसे घेरकर ताबड तोड लाठिया बरसानी शुरू कर दीं। तब कहीं जा कर वह नरभेडिया काबू में आया। आनन-फानन में उसके हाथ और पांव रस्सियों से जकड दिये गये। तब भी, उसके पंजे और दांत इस बुरी तरह से चलते रहे कि कई गांव वालों के चेहरों और शरीर पर खरोंचें पड गयीं और खून बहने लगा। गांववालों ने उसके बंधे हुए हाथ और पेरौं के बीच बांस डाला और कांवर की तरह उसे उठा लिया। वे उसे जॉन मूर के पास ले गये।

बेहद तेज बदबू आ रही थी उस नरभेडिये के शरीर से। जॉन मूर के साथ आये कुत्ते भी उससे कतरा कर दूर भाग गये। जॉन मूर ने गांववालों से कहा कि वे नर-भेडिये के हाथ और पांव खोल दें।

नर भेडिये की कमर में एक जंजीर डालकर उसे एक खूंटे से बांध दिया गया। उसके हाथ और पांव खोल दिये गये। बंधन मुक्त हो जाने पर वह नरभेडिया अपने हाथ और पैर समेट कर कुत्तों की तरह लेट गया। जटाओं की तरह बढे हुए उसके बाल कंधों तक झूल आये थे। उसकी टांगे और बांहे पतली थीं और उन पर उभरी नसों के बीच बेशुमार खरोंचे पडी थीं उसका पेट फूला हुआ था। उसके अगले दांत घिसे हुए थे। लेकिन दाढे मजबूत थी। पशु की देह पर मानव चेहरेवाले उस नरभक्षी की पूंछ भर नहीं थी। बाकी समूची प्रकृति भेडिये जैसी ही प्रतीत होती थी।

जॉन मूर उसे अपने बंगले में ले आया। वहां मिट्टी के तेल का लैंप जल रहा था। जलती हुई रोशनी देख कर वह नरभेडिया बिचका और एक कोने में गुडमुडी हो कर पडा रहा। लेकिन चेहरे पर छायी बेचैनी से साफ जाहिर हो रहा था कि रोशनी उसे उच्छी

नहीं लग रही थी। अंततः उसे बाहर बरामदे में कुत्तों के पास बांध दिया गया।

और वह नायक बन गया

जॉन मूर को उस नर भेडिये की उम्र दस बारह वर्ष से अधिक की नहीं जान पडी। उसका कद 127 से.मी. था। उसके घुटनों, पैरों के तलवों और कोहनियों तथा हथेली की त्वचा बडी खख्त थी। तय था कि यह प्रातः कोहनियों और घुटनों के बल चलता था, कभी-कभी खडा हो कर भागता भी था और फिर पंजों के बल चलने लगता था।

नरभेडिये के पकडे जाने की खबर पा कर कर्नल विलियम स्लीमैन जबलपुरसे संत बावडी आये। उन्होंने लेफ्टिनेंट जॉन मूर को बधाई दी और उसे नरभेडिये को गौर से देखा। उन्हें लगा कि जरूर कोई मादा भेडिया किसी शिशु को उठा कर ले गयी होगी, जहां भेडियों की संगत में उस शिशु का विकास हुआ होगा। भेडियों के साथ रहते-रहते वह खुद भी भेडिया बन गया था और उन्ही के लिए शिकार भी करने लगा था वह, अपहरण की आड में।

विलियम स्लीमैन ने उसके बाल मुंडवाये। अपने निरीक्षण में वे उसे नहलाने के लिए नाले पर भी ले गये, लेकिन पानी देखकर वह विदका। तीन आदमियों ने जब उसे जबरन पानी में ढकेला, तो वह तत्काल बाहर निकल आया और दांत बाहर निकाल कर गुर्राने लगा।

विलियम स्लीमैन को एक तरकीब सूझी। भेडिये जैसे कद्दावर एक बडे कुत्ते को उस नरभेडिये के करीब नहलाया जाने लगा। यह देख कर नरभेडिया भी नहाने लगा। लेकिन उस नरभेडिये को जब एक मादा भेडिया की खाल दिखायी गयी, तो एकाएक वह उत्तेजित हो उठा। उस खाल को उलट-पलट कर उसने कई दफा सूंघा और फिर इतनी जोर से चीखा कि लोगों के दिल दहल गये। ये चीखे गीदडों की चीखों से बहुत मिलती-जुलती थी, लिहाजा उसका नाम ही 'सियार' रख दिया गया।

'सियार' दिन भर सोता रहता, लेकिन रात को वह बुरी तरह से बेचैन हो उठता। वह पुलाव से मांस के टुकडे चुन लेता, कच्चा मांस वह बडे स्वाद के साथ खाता। सूंघने की उसकी शक्ति इतनी

तीव्र थी कि काफी दूर पडी हुई एक मरी हुई भैंस तक पहुंचने के लिए उसने अपनी जंजीरें तोडनी शुरू कर दी थीं।

नर भेडिये में फिर बुद्धि भी विकसित होती नजर आने लगी। उसने गोंड भीलों की भाषा के कुछ शब्द भी सीख लिये और उस भाषा में बात करने और समझने के लायक बन गया। कुत्तों को जब गोश्त के टुकडे खाने के दिए दिये जाते, तो वह उनके पास बैठा रहता।, और जिन कुत्तों को उसने अपना मित्र बनाया था, उनके लिए उस गोश्त में से बोटियां बीन-बीन कर मित्र कुत्तों के सामने रखता जाता। थोडे ही दिनों में उसने लंगोटी पहनना भी शुरू कर दिया।

नरभेडियां 'सियार' को देखने सुदूर होशंगाबाद और नागपुर तक से लोग आने लगे। स्त्रियों ने उसकी पूजा करनी शुरू कर दी। वे उसके सामने दूध और नारियल का ढेर लगा देतीं। वे उसके सामने दूध और नारियल का ढेर लगा देती। लेकिन वह उनकी तरफ देखता भी नहीं था। बच्चों को देखते ही उसकी आदिम हिंश्र प्रवृत्ति जाग उठती और उसकी आंखें वहशत से चमकने लगतीं। स्पष्ट था कि अपनी भेडिया-सौंगनी के साथ न सिर्फ उसने मानव-शिशुओं का मांस चखा था, अपितु उसकी खातिर बच्चे भी उठाये थे।

जॉन मूर को उसकी गतिविधियों देखकर यह समझने में देर नहीं लगी कि उसके पैरो के रहस्यमय निशान एकाएक ही गायब क्यो हो जाते थे। जब वह नरभेडिया अपनी कोहनियों और घुटनों के बल चलता हुआ अचानक ही खडा हो जाता था, तो उसके पांव के निशान दूसरे मनुष्यों के कदमों के निशानों में घुल मिल जाते थे। सरपंच भीकन साव ने अपनी आंखों से जिस पिशाच को पहले कुत्ता और फिर आदमी बनते देखा था, वह यही नरभेडिया 'सियार' था।

'सियार' को विलियम स्लीमैन अपने साथ लखनऊ ले गये, जहां से उसे ईसाई धर्मप्रचारकों के पास भेज दिया गया। बाद में इसी 'सियार' पर प्रख्यात कथाकार रूडयार्ड किपलिंग ने अपनी मशहूर कहानी 'मोगली' की रचना की। इस नरराक्षस के बारे में किपलिंग ने भारी जानकारियां उस समय एकत्र की थीं। जब वे मध्यभारत की देवास रियासत में थे।

(विलियम स्लीमैन लिखित 'द रेम्ब्लेस ऐड रिकलैक्शंस' में संकलित 'द मैन ईटर 'सियार' ऑफ संत बावडी के आधार पर)

रोमांचक

संत बावड़ी का वह मानवभक्षी नरभेड़िया

□ कैलाश नारद

गुत्थियां उलझतीं ही गयीं

खबरदार ! उसे जिंदा ही पकड़ना है

लेकिन हत्यारा कौन था ?

जॉन मूर संजीदा रहा आया। उसे न जाने क्यों ऐसा महसूस हुआ था कि सरपंच के कथन में सच्चाई थी। उसने अपने अर्दली अब्दुल रहमान को अपने पास बुलाया और उसे जमीन पर घुटनों और कोहुनियों के बल चलने के लिए कहा। अब्दुल रहमान उसी मुद्रा में जमीन पर चला, और इस तरह चलने से जो निशान धूल पर बने, वे बहुत कुछ उन रहस्यमय चिह्नों जैसे ही थे। जॉन मूर की आंखें चमक उठीं।

"ऐसे ही निशान गांव से बाहर जंगल में बने शिव-मंदिर के भी पास मैंने अपनी आंखों से देखे हैं, साहब," श्रीकल साव ने जॉन मूर से कहा।

संत वाचली से समझ में आ कि बी. मी. मूर, घनघोर जंगल में एक पहाड़ी नाले के किनारे सदियों पुराना एक शिव मंदिर बना हुआ था। उसका शिखर और बुर्ज टूट गये थे, सिर्फ कंगूर बचा रह गया था। दिन की रोशनी में भी यह बीहड़ बेहद भयावना प्रतीत होता था। लोग वहां से निकलने में कतराते थे।

जॉन मूर के साथ आये सिपाहियों ने शिवमंदिर के इर्द-गिर्द घेरा डाल दिया। वहां की जमीन दलदली थी और उस पर वे रहस्यमय चिह्न बखूबी नजर आ रहे थे। उनके साथ-साथ एक मेंढ़िये के पैरों के निशान भी गीली जमीन पर अंकित थे। शिवमंदिर के आसपास गहरा सन्नाटा था। जब हवा चलती, तो वहां उगी घास और झुरमुटों में सरसराहट होती, फिर सब खामोश हो जाता। सिपाहियों ने उन झुरमुटों में पत्थर फेंके, लेकिन कोई हलचल नहीं हुई। जॉन मूर मंदिर के प्रवेश द्वार की तरफ बढ़ा।

सर्वप्रथम सूना था। वहां सिर्फ टूटा हुआ शिवलिंग और संकित वेदी मौजूद थी और था गहरा अंधेरा। मशाल जला कर वहां रोशनी की गयी, लेकिन भीतर कोई भी नजर नहीं आया। जॉन मूर और सिपाही बाहर निकल आये। तभी मंदिर की उत्तरी दीवार के पास एक पत्थर पर वह की ताजी बूंदें और मानव-केशों का एक गुच्छा एक सिपाही को दिखाई दिया। वहां, ऊपर मंदिर की मेहराब वह गयी थी और उसकी दीवार अन्दर से ऐसी गिरी थी कि वहां एक गुफा-सी बन गयी थी। दीवार पर भी वह के कुछ छींटे गांववालों की नजरों आये।

सत्यरों पर भ‍य कर कुछ लोग टूटी हुई मेहराब के पास पहुंचे, उन्होंने उस गुफा में जैसे ही झांकना चाहा, भीतर से निकला कर कोई बड़ी तेजी से उन पर झपटा।

वह एक मेंढ़िया था। मूरी तरह से गुर्रा रहा था वह। इसके पहले कि वह किसी की क्षति पहुंचाता, जॉन मूर की पिस्तौल से गोली निकली और मुत मेंढ़िया जमीन पर आ गिरा। लेफ्टिनेंट जॉन मूर ने देखा, उसके मुंह में खून लगा हुआ था। गुफा में शिकार की अधखायी लाश पड़ी थी। उसका पेट फाड़ डाला गया था और खून बहे से टूट कर खुल रही थी। लेकिन उसकी बांह पर किसी आदमी के दांतों के चिह्न मौजूद थे।

कौन था वह नरराक्षस? क्या सचमुच वही, जिसे सरपंच श्रीकल साव ने अपनी आंखों से देखा था? लेकिन मेंढ़िये की उस अंधियारी, मयानक गुफा में वह क्या करने आया था?

मंदिर के पिछवाड़े उगे बने झुरमुट पहाड़ी नाले तक पहुंच गये थे। जॉन मूर के साथ आये सिपाहियों ने बड़ी तेजी से उन झुरमुटों में पत्थर फेंकने शुरू कर दिये।

इस सामूहिक अभियान का अनुकूल परिणाम नजर आया। जल्दी ही पानी साहियों में डूबका हुआ वह नर-राक्षस उन्हें मिल गया। सिपाहियों और गांववालों ने उसे घेर लिया और करछे तान कर वे उसकी ओर बढ़ने लगे। तभी जॉन मूर चिल्लाया, "खबरदार, उसे जिंदा ही पकड़ना है।"

वह एक नर-मेंढ़िया था—प्रकृति की ऐसी अनूठी कृति, जिसे जॉन मूर पहली दफा देख रहा था। ईस्ट इंडिया कंपनी के उस कितनाें अफसर के लिए वह एक अनोखा अनुभव था।

अपने को घिरा हुआ पा कर उस नरमेंढ़िये ने भाग निकलने की कोशिश की। जब सिपाही उसके काफी करीब पहुंच गये, तो उनमें से दो सिपाहियों पर वह नर-मेंढ़िया पूरी शक्ति के साथ टूट पड़ा और अपनी बुरी तरह से बढ़े हुए नाखूनों से उसने उनके चेहरों को नोच लिया और तीसरे सिपाही के कंधे पर इस बुरी तरह से दांत गड़ाये कि वहां से गोश्त का एक टुकड़ा ही कट कर अलग हो गया।

सिपाहियों और गांववालों ने उसे घेर कर तावड़-तोड़ लाठियां बरसानी शुरू कर दीं। तब कहीं जा कर वह नरमेंढ़िया काबू में आया। आनन-फानन में उसके हाथ और पांव रस्सियों से जकड़ दिये गये। तब भी, उसके पंजे और दांत इस बुरी तरह से चलते रहे कि कई गांववालों के चेहरों और शरीर पर खरोंचें पड़ गयीं और खून बहने लगा। गांववालों ने उसके बंधे हुए हाथ और पैरों के बीच बांस डाला और कांवर की तरह उसे उठा लिया। वे उसे जॉन मूर के पास ले गये।

मेहुत तेज बदबू आ रही थी उस नरमेंढ़िये के शरीर से। जॉन मूर के साथ आये कुछ सिपाही उससे दूर भाग गये। जॉन मूर ने गांववालों से कहा कि वे नर-मेंढ़िये के हाथ और पांव खोल दें।

नरमेंढ़िये की कमर में एक जंजीर डाल कर उसे एक खूंटे से बांध दिया गया। उसके हाथ और पांव खोल दिये गये, बंधन मुक्त ही जाने पर वह नरमेंढ़िया अपने हाथ और पैर समेट कर कुत्तों की तरह लेट गया। जटाओं की तरह बढ़े हुए, उसके बाल कंधों तक झुल आये थे। उसकी टांगें और बांहें पतली थीं और उन पर उभरी नसों के बीच बेशुमार खरोंचें पड़ी थीं। उसका पेट कूसा हुआ था। उसके बगले दांत घिसे हुए थे, लेकिन वर्ई मजबूत थी। पशु की देह पर मानव चेहरेवाले उस नरमक्षी की पूछ मर नहीं थी, बाकी समूची प्रकृति मेंढ़िये जैसी ही प्रतीत होती थी।

जॉन मूर उसे अपने अंगने में ले आया। वहां मिट्टी के तेल का लैंप जल रहा था। जलती हुई रोशनी देख कर वह नरमेंढ़िया चिंका और एक कोने में गुड़मुड़ी हो कर पड़ रहा। लेकिन, उसके चेहरे पर छायी बेचैनी से साफ जाहिर हो रहा था कि रोशनी उसे अच्छी नहीं लग रही थी। अंततः उसे शहर न रामदे में कुत्तों के पास बांध दिया गया।

और वह नायक बन गया

जॉन मूर को उस नरमेंढ़िये की उम्र दस-बारह वर्ष से अधिक की नहीं जान पड़ी। उसका कद—१२७ सें. मी. था। उसके घुटनों, पैरों के तलवों और कोहुनियों तथा हथेली की त्वचा बड़ी सख्त थी। तय था कि वह प्रायः कोहुनियों और घुठनों के बल चलता था, कभी-कभी सक्त हो कर भगता भी था और फिर पंजों के बल चलने लगता था।

लेफ्टिनेंट जॉन मूर, को उस नरभक्षी को पकड़वा कर अपने अंगने पर ले आवे थे।

नरमेंढ़िये के पकड़े जाने की खबर पर कर कर्नल विलियम स्लीमन जबलपुर से संत वाचली आये। उन्होंने लेफ्टिनेंट जॉन मूर की बधाई दी और उस नरमेंढ़िये को चीर से देखा। उन्हें लगा कि जरूर कोई मादा मेंढ़िया किसी शिशु को उठा कर ले गयी होगी, जहां मेंढ़ियों की संगत में उस शिशु का विकास हुआ होगा। मेंढ़ियों के साथ रहते-रहते वह खुद भी मेंढ़िया बन गया था और उन्हीं के लिए शिकार भी करने लगा था वह, अपनूल की आयु में।

विलियम स्लीमन ने उसके बाल मुंड़वाये। अपनी निगरानी में वे उसे नहलाने के लिए नाले पर भी ले गये, लेकिन पानी देख कर वह बिदका। तीन आदमियों ने जब उसे जबरन पानी में डकेला, तो वह तत्काल बाहर निकल आया और शोर शराबे बाहर निकास कर नुदीने लगा।

विलियम स्लीमन की एक तरकीब चूमी। मेंढ़िये जैसे बड़बड़र एक बड़े कुत्ते को उस नरमेंढ़िये के करीब ही नहलाया जाने लगा। यह देख कर वह नरमेंढ़िया भी नहाने लगा। लेकिन उस नरमेंढ़िये की जब एक मादा मेंढ़िया की बात दिखायी गयी, तो एकाएक वह चलेजित हो उठा। उस चाल को उछल-पल्ट कर उसने कई दफा सूंघा और फिर इतनी और से चीखा कि सोंगों के दिल दहल गये। वे चीखें गीदड़ों की चीखों से बहुत मिलती-जुलती थीं, लिहाजा उसका नाम ही 'सियार' रख दिया गया।

'सियार' दिन मर सोता रहता, लेकिन रात को वह बुरी तरह से बेचैन ही उठता। वह पुलाव से मांस के टुकड़े चुन लेता, कच्चा मांस वह बड़े स्वाद से साथ खाता। सूंघने की उसकी शक्ति इतनी तीव थी कि काफी दूर पड़ी हुई एक मरी हुई मैंस तक पहुंचने के लिए उसने अपनी जंजीर तोड़नी शुरू कर दी थी।

नरमेंढ़िये में फिर बुद्धि भी विकसित होती नजर आने लगी। उसने गोंद मीलों की भाषा के कुछ शब्द भी सीख लिये और उस भाषा में बात करने और समझने के लायक बन गया। कुत्तों को जब गोश्त के टुकड़े खाने के लिए दिये आते, तो वह उनके पास बैठा रहता। और जिन कुत्तों को उसने अपना मित्र बनाया था, उनके लिए उस गोश्त में वे बोटियां बीन-बीन कर जिन कुत्तों के सामने रखता जाता। चौरे ही दिनों में उसने लंगोटी पहनना भी शुरू कर दिया।

नरमेंढ़िया 'सियार' को देखने भूरर हीराबाद और नागपुर तक से लोग आने लगे। स्त्रियों में उसकी पूजा करनी शुरू कर दी। वे उसके सामने धूप और लोबान जलाती थीं, लेकिन वह उनकी तरफ देखता भी नहीं था। बच्चों को देखते ही उसकी आदिम हिंस्र प्रवृत्ति जाग उठती और उसको आंखें महुसव से चमकने लगतीं। लगता था कि अपनी मेंढ़िया-मांगनी के साथ न सिर्फ उसने मानव-शिशुओं का मांस चखा था, उसके लिए अपितु उसकी शातिर बच्चे भी उठायें थे।

जॉन मूर को उसकी गतिविधियां देख कर वह समझने में देर नहीं लगी कि उसके पैरों के रहस्यमय निशान एकाएक ही गायब क्यों हो जाते थे। अब वह नरमेंढ़िया अपनी कोहुनियों और घुटनों के बल चलता हुआ अचानक ही खड़ा हो जाता था, तो उसके पांव के निशान दूसरे मनुष्यों के कदमों के निशानों में घुल-मिल जाते थे। सरपंच श्रीकल साव ने अपनी आंखों से जिस पिशाच को पहले कुत्ता और फिर आदमी बनते देखा था, वह वही नरमेंढ़िया 'सियार' था।

'सियार' को विलियम स्लीमन अपने साथ नागपुर ले गये, जहां से उसे ईसाई धर्मप्रचारकों के पास भेज दिया गया। बाद में इसी 'सियार' पर प्रख्यात कथाकार रड्यार्ड किपलिंग ने अपनी मशहूर कहानी 'मोगली' की रचना की। इस नरराक्षस के बारे में किपलिंग ने सारी जानकारियां उस समय एकत्र की थीं, जब वे मध्यभारत की देवाछ रियासत में थे।

■ ■ ■

(विलियम स्लीमन लिखित 'अ रैम्बल एंड रिकलेक्शंस' में संकलित 'अ मैन ईटर सियार आंफ संत वाचली' के आधार पर)

True Story of Mowgli being Caught

Dharmyug: 27 June 1982,
Published by Willium Sleeman in London
Man-eater, Wolf boy of Sant Bavadi
* Kailash Narad
(English Translation of Article on Dharmyug)

Thriller

Man eater wolf boy of Sant Bavadi

Vast Teak forest spreading down from Satpuda hills to south wards, very Dense, Impassable and its roof is visible but it is scattered, and Jabalpur -Nagpur highway is seen in-between, Village Sant Babadi is still there but buses do not stop there.

Sant Babadi, a Sleeping village, slum of five hundred fifty houses with trees of Neem and Mahua, was exciting in whole of Narmada -Sagar area during time of East India company for unusual and weird cases and even Willium Sleeman, the unparallel hero to repression of Thugs was restless due to the happenings of Sant Bavdi village and in the year 1831 he himself reached Sant Babadi village covering distance of eighty four miles (135 km) on horseback so that he could study himself on ground about satanic type of events, but after staying there for three day and three nights he could not find anything, then Willian Sleeman left his subordinate Mr. John Moor in Sant Babadi Village and he return back to Jabalpur. He instructed John Moor to immediately inform him of any mystery being solved.

What was happening in Sant Bavadi village?

Nineteenth century India of Dark age was full of heinous crimes by historical cruel killers and Thugs. Chaotic elements have the experience of choking of throat of their prey by yellow scarf and they are blood thirsty. This was the most disgraced period in the history of East India company when the area between Ganga -Yamuna river and area between Narmada -Kaveri river was full of unknown and unidentified dead bodies.

William Sleeman was the first British officer who raised the most powerful voice against the cruelty of Thugs. It was due to his effort that the then Governor General of India Lord William Benting has created Thuggi eradication department under his leadership and it's headquarter was Jabalpur. Jhon Moor was one of his loyal companion posted in Narmada -Sagar landscape. He was in charge of Seoni-Balaghat and doing repression of Thuggs.

Sant Bavadi village situated between Jabalpur and Nagpur road was hunting ground of Thuggs and it was so infamous that people named him Thug Bavadi. In last one and half month thirty two persons have been missing and it was presumed that infamous Thuggs were behind their murder after robbing them and disappearing their dead bodies.

Lieutenant Jhon Moor Started investigation but it was so complicated that he stay confused. Missing persons were neither rich nor they were religious tourist going for long distances which are normally easy prey of Thuggs. On the contrary among missing persons most of the unfortunate were ladies and children and on this point Jhon Moor was confused. Killing of women and children was forbidden in the code of conduct of Thuggs, and the other three persons who were missing one of them was cattle herder and two were musician, sitar and Pakhawas players, who were returning from Chhapara after a marriage ceremony and were suddenly missing. In the code of conduct of Thuggs killing of cattle herder and musician were forbidden. If these thirty two unfortunate persons were not killed by Thuggs then who was behind disappearance of them and what was the objective of it.

Complications were more confusing?

Doubt of Jhon Moor was on the Bhils living in nearby hillocks. But their own women and children were missing and there were frightening terror among them. They were badly scared and were thinking that some satanic power was behind these diabolic activity. To control these epiophilic power relatives of missing persons on the advice of village tantric have given sacrifice of Chicken and male goat, but still violence did not stop.

Jhon Moor thought that it may be the act of any tiger but his doubt was unfounded because there was no information of any tiger in the area neither tigers pug marks were seen.

Then Jhon Moor thought that this may be act of hyena and wolves'. The way people were missing this was sure work of wolves. Those unfortunate were missing were lifted in third pah of night from their veranda and even their bones were not found, Where lion and tiger leave bones of prey but hyena and wolf digest bones also. They are fond of chewing bones but there were neither proof of missing persons were killed by hyena and wolves. Because in whole area Jhon Moor did not find any foot print of wolf and any such animal.

Some peculiar marks were found near houses of missing persons which further created confusion of solders of East India Company. They were the mark of paws but of which animal? They were four circular marks very deep and behind them there were such marks which were made by broad Brush. These Marks were clearly seen upto one or two furlongs and then they suddenly disappear in such places where there is no scrub, neither forest nor a river or hillock. Those peculiar marks were found disappeared in plain ground.

Wolf man: Imitated image by Vishnu Agnihotri of the sketch made by Lieutenant Jhon Moor

Such marks and their uncertainty has boiled the whole village. Villagers were of the view that those which are missing must have been killed by bad sprit and those peculiar marks were of that bad sprit opposite foot who comes in dark night slowly and lifts his prey.

Then one night a boy from hut of a villager was missing. Boy was sleeping with his mother when in the midnight herd rustle around her and till she is awake the boy was missing. This incidence happened inside hut but the door was open. Embraced mother came out thinking the child might have fallen outside but the child was not there.

Bewildered, mother running here and there madly for his child, other people came out after hearing noise. There were no pug mark of any wild animal but the blood was scattered all over. It was clear that the child has been murdered.

Be Watchful? He has to be caught alive.
But who is the killer?
Jhon Moor along with hunting dogs and villagers on the same night searched sant Bavadi village and miles away but could not find any sign of killer. Near hut he found same mysterious marks the same four circular, deep marks two in front and two in back 40 centimeter apart and, back pug mark were relatively bigger in size than fore marks, from the front marks brush type marks were linked and a stripe of dirt was there in their back. Satanic marks after some distance were disappeared.

Terror in the village has been increased due to this incident, and then after two days one goldsmith was also missing from his house in the same way. Then the whole atmosphere was woke up. Trouble of Jhon Moor has increased after this incidence. He could not understand how to cope up with this unknown and mysterious killer.

In the afternoon when he was sitting in the veranda, one old man came to him. Jhon moor recognized him. He was the Village Head (Sarpanch) of Sant Bavadi Bhikan Sao. He came with very sensitive information. Bhikan Sao told him that he has seen that demon last night himself, he was first looking like man then he became dog like and he disappeared suddenly looking at him.

Other officers of East India Company sitting with Jhon Moor were laughing hearing the talk of Bhikan Sao but Jhon Moor was serious. He doesn't know but felt truth in the tale of Sarpanch. He called his orderly Abdul Rahman and told him to walk on knees and elbow. Abdul Rahman walked in that position in the field and the marks in the dust were similar to that of mysterious marks found earlier. John Moor eyes were shinning.

Bhikan Sao told Jhon Moor that he has seen similar marks near Shiva temple out side village.

About two kilometer away from Sant Bavadi Village in dense forest in the bank of a hilly bore there was a century old Shiva temple. Its peak and turret were fallen and only ruins were remaining. In the day time also that rugged area was very horrifying. Solders of Jhon Moor encircled the Shiva temple. There the land was swampy and those mysterious marks were clearly visible. Along with those marks pugmarks of a wolf was also seen which was marked in swampy soil. Near Shiva temple it was deep silence and when wind were blowing then there were rustling sound in scrub and in grasses and then every things become silent. Solders thrown stones in those clumps but there was no movement, John Moor extended to the entrance of the temple.

Central of temple was empty and there was broken Shiva linga and broken Yagya vedi and was deep darkness. Then the torch was lit up. But nobody was there inside. John Moor and solders came out. Then in the north side wall of temple fresh blood and hair of human being was seen by one solder. In the upper part of temple arch and wall were so fallen as is like cave. Blood were scene in the wall by some villagers.

Some people after stepping over stones went near broken arches and as soon as they tried to bark inside something swiftly came out from inside and jumped over them. It was a wolf and he was growling very badly. Before it can hurt anybody Jhon moor fired from his pistol and wolf was fallen dead on the ground. Lieutenant Jhon Moor saw blood in his mouth and in the cave half eaten dead body of goldsmith was lying there. His stomach was open and his arms broken arm was swinging from his shoulder but in his arm there were marks of human teeth.

Who was that devil man? What if he is the same man which Bhikan Sao seen by his own eyes. But why he came in the dark cave of wolf?

In the back of temple dense scrub forest was spread up to Stream. Solders came with Jhon Moor started pelting stones very swiftly towards those clumps.

Due to this combined effort favorable result came out. Soon they found that devil from the dense shrubs that was hiding there. Solders and villagers encircled him and by pointing spears towards him started towards him and only then Jhon Moor shouted "Beware, he has to be caught live"

He was a Wolf man, Jhon Moor was seeing for the first time this unique work of nature. This was the unique experience for British officer of East India Company.

After he found himself encircled, wolf man tried to run away. When soldiers came close to him that wolf man with full strength attacked two solders and from big nails he screw their faces and he bitten by his teeth very badly to the third one in his shoulder that slice of flesh came out.

Solders and villagers encircled him and started beating him by sticks, and then only wolf man is brought under control. Very promptly his feet and hands were clamped with ropes. Then also from his claws and teeth many villagers face and body got scratches and blood started oozing. Villager put bamboos in between his hands and feet and lifted him like kanwad. They took him before Jhon Moor.

Very strong stench was coming from the body of that wolf man. Dogs came with Jhon Moor also got away scared by him.

Jhon Moor told villagers that they should open his hand and feet. Wolf man was chained in his waist and tied in a peg. After being freed from bondage that wolf man lied down by crimping his hands and feet like dog. His hairs were coiled and hanging down shoulders. His legs and arms were thin and over their nerves countless scratches were seen and his stomach was swollen. His fore teeth were worn out but his molar teeth were strong. The wolf man is in the body of animal with human face except without tail. Rest of his whole nature was like wolf.

Jhon Moor brought him in his Bungalow where a lamp of oil was burning. Seeing the light of lamp wolf man was scared and lying in a corner like a bundle. But restlessness seen in his face was clearly shows that he did not like light. At last he was tied in the veranda near dogs.

And He became the Hero.

As per Jhon moor the age of wolf man was not more than ten to twelve years. His height was 127 centimeter. The skin of his legs, soles of feet, elbow and skin of palm was very tough. It was clear that he was walking with his elbow and knees in the morning and sometimes he runs after standing like a man and again he moves on his paws.

After hearing the news of wolf man being caught Colonel William Sleeman came to village Sant Bavadi. He congratulated Lieutenant Jhon Moor and saw intently that wolf man. He thought that definitely some female wolf has lifted any small boy and on the company of wolves that boy was brought up. Due to living with wolves he himself become wolf and doing hunting for them on the pretext of kidnapping.

William Sleeman got his hair removed. On his inspection he took him to the river Streme for bathing but he stopped looking to water, when three persons threw him in water he came out immediately out of water and started growling with teeth being taken out.

William Sleeman found a trick. One big Dog looking like big wolf was being bathed near that wolf man. Looking to this Wolf man also started bathing. But when this wolf man was shown a skin of dead female wolf then he was suddenly agitated. He smelled that skin many times after overturning, and then he screamed very high that people were scared. These screams were similar to that of a jackal and hence he was named as jackal.

Jackal used to sleep during daytime but in the night he becomes restless. He used to take out pieces of meat from Pulav, and he liked raw meat with great taste. His smell power was so powerful that he started breaking his chain to reach a dead buffalo lying at far away distance.

Then some intelligence was seen developing in wolf man. He did learn few words of Gondi and Bhil tribes' dialect and in that language he was able to speak and understand. And when dogs were served pieces of meats then he used to sit near them and he gives pieces of meat to those dogs whom he developed friendship. After some time he started bearing loincloth.

To see Wolf man "jackal" lot of people from faraway Hoshangabad and Nagpur were coming. Woman started worshiping him. They keep milk and coconut before him but he could not see that thing. His primitive violence nature was aroused after seeing the children and his eyes were burning with savage. It was clear that he has eaten human child flesh but also kidnapped children.

Jhon Moor looking to his activity could understand without any delay that why mysterious marks of his feet used to disappear suddenly? When that wolf man while walking in his knees and elbow suddenly starts walking after standing then his pug marks were dissolved with the feet marks of other human beings. Sarpanch Bhikan Sao saw that devil from his own eyes that became dog first and then man was this same wolf man "Jackal".

"Jackal" was taken by William Sleeman to Lukhnow from where he was sent to Christian Missionaries. Later on Renowned writer Rudyard Kippling has written story of Mowgli based on this "Jackal". Kippling has collected all information on this wolf man Jackal when he was working in Dewas Principality of Central India.

(On the basis of writing of William Sleeman in "The Rambles and Recollection "in an article "The Man Eater Siyar of Sant Bavadi")

Publicity for Making Pench Tiger Reserve a popular Destination:
Now Mowgli has become USP for marketing our National Park as a popular destination for sighting of Tiger and other wild animals.

Mowgli and The Jungle Book is famous word wide and in India also due to TV serial The Jungle Book, so people started coming to this park from India and abroad.

This created demand for Hotels which was well taken by market forces and private hotels and lodges were come up very fast.

After publicity in local news paper, it came into the notice of India today Magazine and a correspondent Ms. Prerana Bindra a known wild life activist came with a photographer to see the area of the Mowgli and places mentioned in The area of the Jungle Book and Ms. Prerana Bindra wrote a beautiful article about this area as the area of the "The Jungle book" which was published in Jan 2002 in India today

Year Wise Tourist Influx and Revenue

Year	Indian	Foreigner	Total	Revenue
1997–98	988	0	988	42995
1998–99	1156	14	1170	55692
99–2000	1329	4	1333	67400
2000–01	5274	14	5288	275170
2001–02	10449	39	10488	600110
2002–03	18170	138	18308	1041908
2003–04	20240	568	20808	1284602
2004–05	23336	1160	24496	3398830
2005–06	30459	1687	32146	5372220
2006–07	44061	1495	45556	10399679
2007–08	50897	3309	54206	8597598
2008–09	59303	5168	64471	11256880
2009–10	47758	4796	52554	10398096

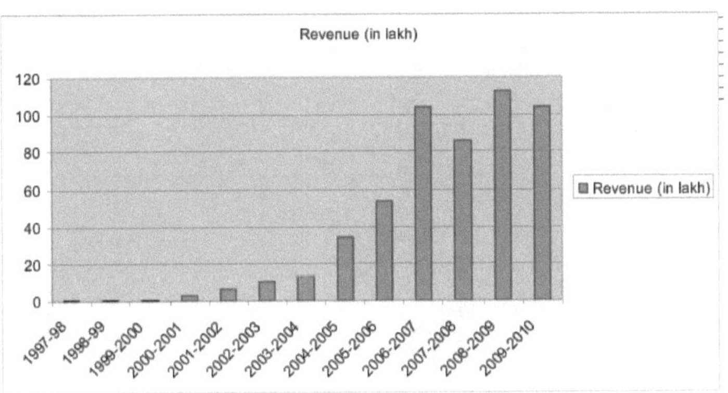

Year Wise Revenue

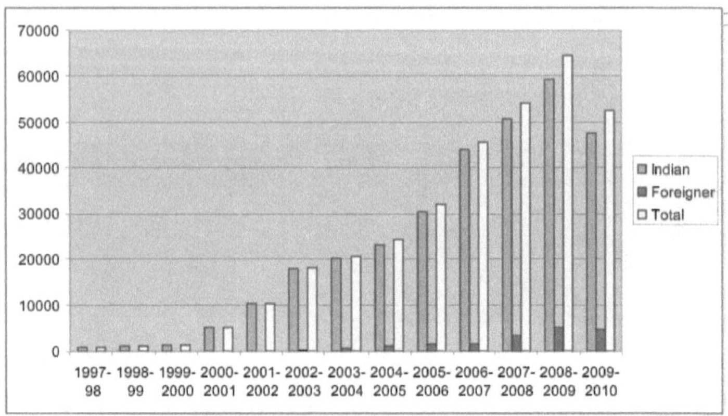

पर्यटक की संख्या एवं उनसे प्राप्त आय की जानकारी

वर्ष	पर्यटकों की संख्या			पर्यटन द्वारा प्राप्त आय (रूपये में)
	भारतीय	विदेशी	योग	
2000-01	5274	14	5288	275170
2001-02	10449	39	10488	600110
2002-03	18170	138	18308	1041908
2003-04	20240	568	20808	1284602
2004-05	23336	1160	24496	3398830
2005-06	30459	1687	23146	5372220
2006-07	14061	1495	45556	10399679
2007-08	50857	3309	54206	8597598
2008-09	59303	5168	64471	11256880
2009-10	47758	4796	52554	10398096
2010-11	60038	5421	65459	18080606
2011-12	63802	6282	70084	19238430
2012-13	44407	5043	49450	13640176
2013-14	46602	5502	52104	19555350
2014-15	54771	5617	60388	22877920
2015-16	68217	7024	75241	31347400
2016-17	70730	7505	78235	27430460
2017-18	74197	8427	82624	28808123

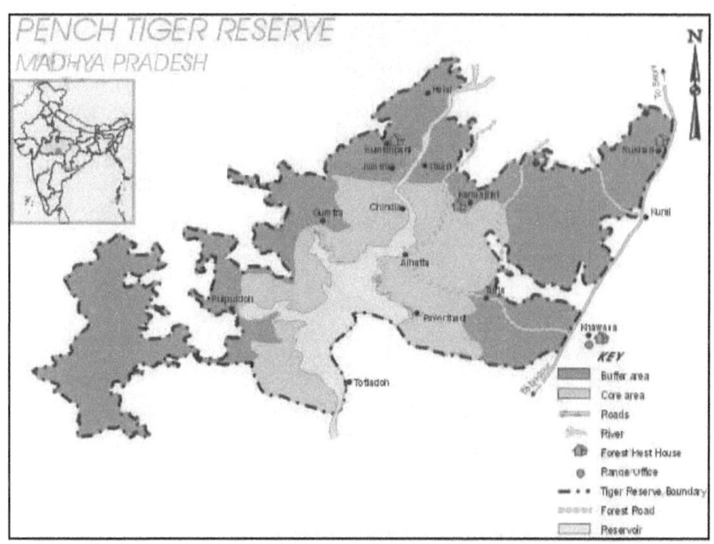

Census (2015 to 2018)

Popu. Estimate of prey species in Pench TR
Buffer - 470.06 Sq.Km.

Species	2015 Summer	2016 Winter	2017 Winter	2018 Winter
Chital	5093	4999	4547	4433
Sambar	539	2397	839	1635
Bluebull	3004	1536	2410	1674
Wild boar	8492	8136	4208	4351
Common langur	23571	19330	14520	19154
Peafowl	548	322	161	583
Gaur	814	138	375	511

Census (2014 to 2018)

Popu. Estimate of prey species in Pench TR
Core Area - 411.330 Sq.Km.

Species	2015 Winter	2016 Winter	2017 Winter	2018 Winter
Chital	59330	50820	48751	47973
Sambar	5765	6461	6543	6672
Bluebull	2012	2312	2035	2152
Wild boar	7355	5853	10213	8914
Common langur	46789	37595	27596	29536
Peafowl	1456	2006	735	1549
Gaur	1326	1043	1120	1266

Tiger and Panther Census Pench Tiger Reserve Seoni M.P.

Year	Species	
	Tiger	Panther
2000	46	34
2001	50	29
2002	50	32
2003	55	39
2004	57	39
2005	56	41
2006	*27–39 Adult Tiger in Pench Landscape	-
2007		
2008		
2009		
2010	*65(53–78)Tiger	-

Year	Species	
	Tiger	Panther
2011	*23	-
2012	-	-
2013	**36	-
2014	**43	-

*Figures for 2006 and 2010 are for the Pench landscape that includes Pench Maharashtra

** 2011,2013,2014, Tiger figures are minimum number of tigers found in the core area during yearly camera trap exercise.

*From the year 2006 onwards Tiger census was shifted to new method and earlier one was Pug Mark method. It seems that 2006 census does not give correct figure because in 2010 it is 65 tigers which is twice of 2006. It is clear that pug mark method figure of 56 tiger was correct.

It has boosted more publicity, then it was shown in Aaj tak TV news channel which actually help a lot to inform public at large in India about this popular destination.

In order to make Pench a popular destination in domestic as well as abroad i requested Mr. Suhel Gupta the owner of first hotel in Pench to arrange a workshop of all big and small companies engaged in tourist business in wild area, at Delhi to promote our destination.

Dinner was organized along with presentation about Pench Tiger Reserve, in India International Center attended by around 40 managers of different companies and i advocated about the wilderness beauty of Pench Tiger reserve and about wild animals they can see with photographs and short film made by our daily wage staff.

This was a great success and they promised to send tourist to this new destination. Mowgli land and the area of the jungle book as added advantage to tourist helped in promoting tourism to Pench Tiger Reserve.

My vision about Tourism Promotion Vis-a-Vis wild life Conservation:

I was quite clear that tourism will help conservation because local population being the stakeholders will get lot of employment and due to its popularity Government and Forest department will be keen to help this park in its development.

Kanha and Bandhavgarh Tiger reserve being very old tourist destination has a name in wild tourism circuit also had good film on wild animals found there had been made and being shown in Discovery channel etc. which further attracts tourists from abroad as well as Indian.

But there was no film on Pench Tiger reserve Seoni so i thought to have such a film but it requires huge money which is not possible from state funding.

I talked to one Mr. Suhel Gupta who along with his friends constructed first private hotel named as "Baghvan ", and his associate Mr. Tobi Sing who happens to be international guide to Indian Wild Tourist Destination, to bring film maker on wild animals from abroad to produce good film, and they did bring good photographer from abroad with my help they photographed wild animals and forest of Pench and send proposal and got approval to make film which started since 2006 and in three years they made a film named " Spy in the Jungle" three hour film with latest technology. This film is being shown in Discovery channel which attracted foreign tourists.

This way a film on wild life of Pench was made without state funding and we got Approx. 60 lakh rupees every year from them for elephant they hired and fees of filming this is how you got the publicity done without spending any money rather by earning money. This is a lesson to be learnt by young managers of Park.

Due to publicity few more private hotels have come up there to enhance more tourism. Taj international, Tuli international, Pench jungle camp like hotels with high standard accommodation attracted high value tourists from abroad as well.

In order to boost tourism apart from publicity you must have abundant prey base, variety of wild animals and tiger population which is visible to tourist and that gives reliable mouth to mouth publicity.

Tiger Centric Tourism:
Tourism in wild area is tiger centric. Tourist come here for mostly sighting tiger, once they see it then they feel relieved and pack up to return and if not seen a tiger then they are disappointed and will say park is not good as a destination. Park management try to show tiger as much as possible.

Tiger sighting in M.P. was through sitting in Elephant back. Four person rides at a time and elephant goes as close as 10–15 feet. Two to three elephants are kept surrounding the tiger so that it cannot go away and rest of the available elephants are kept close to the area in nearby road from where tourists go to see tigers.

Process for tiger sighting starts at 4 am when Mahavats go to search elephants inside forest for 2–4 kilometer where they go for grazing as these were left to forest for grazing. This is very dangerous and difficult to move in dark. There are fear of snakes and carnivores like tiger, panther etc., then they bring back elephants and feed them and tie them with ropes and Howdah (castle in the back) then they go again to forest inside to search for tiger movement.

Tiger moves from early morning at 3 am to 7 am and it rest after sun rise so Mahavats have to locate tiger movement before sun rise otherwise it will not be traced. Tiger moves in the morning and due to his presence monkeys and deer give call by which it is located.

At least 4 elephants were needed for this operation and if we have more elephant then we can locate tiger at two places and more number of tourists can be shown. Pench tiger reserve had only 4 tigers where as Kanha Tiger reserve has more than 20 elephants and Bandhavgarh has around 15 elephants. So Kanha and Bandhavgarh make at least 3 groups and tiger were sighted at 3 places and this was main reason to prefer these places.

We always wanted to ask for more elephants to promote our place.

But this way of sighting of tigers from elephant back was very tiring and inhuman to elephants and to Mahavats and staff and it was dangerous for tourist as mishap can happen due to tiger which is very near.

Now this system has been banned since 2014 on the basis of cruelty to elephant and it was bad for tiger also as it has to stopped forcibly and disturbed when on sleep after wandering throughout night for hunting.

Now you have to see it from gypsy and people have to be made aware of looking for whole nature and other animals and birds. Looking tiger in wild condition is more thrilling and this can be improved if water bodies are nearby.

Pench to be a popular Destination for Bird Watching:
Pench Tiger reserve has more than 400 birds also visited by lot number of migratory birds. If you exclude Siberian crane then number of birds found in Pench tiger reserve will

be equal to Bharatpur bird sanctuary which attracts lot of foreign tourists.

Most important birds are racket tailed Dongo, Malabar pied hornbill, grey hornbill, paradise fly catcher, Indian Pitta, coppersmith, vultures, etc.

Among migratory water birds are Pintail, goose, Brahmni duck, Bar headed goose, Nakata, etc.

Pench has to be made popular for bird watching to attract foreign tourist for bird watching.

Large number of butterflies is another attraction for tourist, many endangered butterflies were found here.

Good Tourism Promotes Development of Local Villagers:
Pench is the Success story of Tourism and village development. Prior to the popularity of Pench Tiger Reserve villagers were against Park because due to park so many restrictions were imposed for entree and collection of minor forest produce. Due to enhance tourism villagers were getting employment and price of their land is increase in manifolds. They sold few acres of land adjoining to park and purchased more land away from park. some of the locals got employment as guide, and in Hotel and lodges which came up there. They purchased Gypsies to give park round and getting lot of income.

Shanta Bai a Tribal Lady is the epitome of Successful Tourism:
Shanta Bai a tribal lady came to meet me leading a delegation of villagers complaining about crop raiding by spotted deer in her village Karmajhiri in July 2001 when I had just joined as Field Director Pench Tiger Reserve.

I went to see their farms and almost all Maize crops was grazed by spotted deer. She was telling that we all villagers want to leave this village please help us to settle in other place. We could not take a crop and there is no work in the forest due to Park. National park was declared in the year 1983 -84 but after 16 yrs have passed villagers were aggrieved due to crop loss by wild animals and Govt. was not compensating their losses.

I just said that you people better know how to live in forest area and survive, but was deeply thinking what to do.

After I discovered Mowgli as an USP and Tourist Influx started to increase from 1000 to 11000 and so on people realized potential of tourism.

One day in 2004 Shanta bai came to me when I was staying there to ask for Rupees 25000 rupees loan to construct home stay two room suit to be constructed by her which will be utilized by tourists in case there is no accommodation in forest rest house.

This is called success of Tourism when the lady was earlier telling to relocate entire village but after increase in tourism and scope of employment she wanted to construct home stay rooms and this is the success of tourism potential of Pench and resolving man -animal conflict.

Problems facing the Park and approach to solve in an innovative way

(1) Water Problem:-

Lack of Water in most of the Park and sanctuary area, Though Pench river is flowing in the middle of the park but both side do not have water above soil from the month of November -December, because soil is sandy and water goes down in subsoil in depth so it is not available for drinking water to wild animals.

Due to this most of the wild animal concentrate near Pench river bank in both side and habitat in river banks is overgrazed but other areas are underutilized.

This causes under utilization of most of the area and overutilization of small area in river bank side.

As wild life is concentrated in river bank side and this is mostly in non tourism zone so tourist could not see wild animals properly.

There was only one small tank Sajapani which do not have water after December.

In order to give drinking water to wild animals previously they used to fill cement saucer on road side by water tanker and they have hand pumps to take out water and it goes to a saucer by pipe or a water channel some 100 feet away. Hand pump was operated by daily wagers living in nearby camp.

Water stored in saucer get very hot in summer and it is not drinkable by wild animals.

In tourism zone, pulling of hand pump by a human does not feel like we are in forest and our adventure sprit goes down.

So i designed innovative method for availability of drinking water to wild animals which is perfectly natural by digging jhiriya at suitable places 4–5 feet deep and 4 meter diameter.

Jhiriya should be dug at such places which are in valley, where jamun, Arjun tree is there and where grasses are green and bees seen sitting there. If you dugout 4–5 feet deep, water will come out and this water will be very cool in summer and is natural for wild animals and these are inside forest so here wild animals don't get disturbed by tourists.

We had made more than 100 such jhiriyas at well distributed way in the entire area of tiger reserve. This helped to increase prey base throughout Park.

Forest guard Gautam soni discovered a point in a hillock Khairvanmatta near Raiyakassa where water was seeping very slowly. He made a small Nala bandhan (stream Check Dam) by Pudlling black cotton soil and then diverting seepage water through a pipe to the nala bandhan. This place is called Tumdiair.

There was so much water that 4 feet deep Nala bandhan was full and extra water was diverted through waste bear to second Nala bandhan and then to third bandhan.

This Was so useful for wild life in hillock area where there was no water and they have to travel 3–5 km for drinking water, that we have seen lots of Sambar drinking water as Sambar is mostly found in hills and in dense forests so this water body became the most used one. Tiger, sloth bear etc were found drinking water there.

Gautam Soni Forest Guard name was recommended for out of turn promotion for his contribution to conservation of wild life and creating a water body in hillock area with his innovative skills and he got promotion as forester.

This reward for good work motivated many forest guards and other officers to search, jhiriya site where it can be constructed apart from other good works. This helped to have more than 100 jhiriyas and it solved water problem across the park.

Construction of low cast Nala Bandhan at 1–2 km interval in small Nalas in the month of October -November to stop flowing water at different locations in the same nala. This helps to retain water upto march -April and then jhiriya can be dugout downside of nala bandhan. This work did wonders as far as water availability is concerned and increase in prey base along with its uniform distribution.

Construction of Small tanks in park and sanctuary area:-
Small tanks have been constructed at 3–5 km distances in the area at suitable places in small nalas (stream). Area has acute shortage of water and water was not available over surface after December and there was only one small tank name as Sajapani which do not have water after February, so it was essential to have sufficient water in summer in different part of the tiger reserve in well distributed manner.

It was a huge task as budget was not available for this and with limited budget you cannot do it. Eco development project under GEF funding from World Bank was running since 1997–98 and it was to end in 2003 but there was no budget left for park management as almost all the budget on this has been exhausted in road repair and construction of stop dam etc. Now the Budget left was for eco development in surrounding 99 villages.

World bank officials supervising our project told me that some percent of budget is left to be spend on discretion of Field director.

I used that budget which was approximately 1.75 crores of rupees for construction of 10 small tanks inside tiger reserve and 3 small tanks in three villages for drinking water to village cattle which were stopped entering National park to drink water in Totaladoh dam by constructing cattle proof wall having length of 40 km in the boundary of park. Also Discretionary fund was utilized to construct Cattle proof wall from random rubble along boundary of National Park in Chhindwara side of Park. We constructed approximately 40 km such wall.

State Govt. has for the first time allotted budget for construction of water bodies in PA areas under drought scarcity fund directly to forest Deptt. And we constructed nearly ten more tanks. This resulted in overall proper water management in tiger reserve area and due to that prey base has increased enormously and specially spotted deer population was more than 25000 in the PA.

Under scarcity fund 30% money and 70% cost will be given in the form of Rice or wheat i.e food grain from district authorities. Our staff was not interested to construct dams on these conditions due to formalities and dealing with district authorities probably due to bad experience in the past. But i insisted that i have finalized the sites of all ten tanks so it will be criminal waste not to utilize money first time given for constructing tanks for drinking water to wild animals. Staff was telling that labor is not available then I gave in writing that work will be allotted to all ranges and duty of officers will be given in writing and all officers from forest guard to deputy director will be made responsible to complete the work before rains and C.R. i.e annual appraisal marking will be done looking to their performance in this work which is very important. Those doing 120% will be given A+, 100% A, 80% B, 60%C and down below will be negative marking and I will write to my PCCF to give me marks in CR on the basis of average of all my staff and the result was that we did perform 120% and all the tanks were constructed before rains. What is today in Pench Tiger reserve on water management resulting into highest prey base and highest tiger density is due to this type of hard work done by me and my staff.

Construction of Alikatta tank which is now the lifeline of park was done in three and half month from 5th may to 18 august and due to God blessing there were no rains in the catchment of this dam. Cost of dam was aprox.13 lakh rupees and done under scarcity fund. We feared for early rain in June last week but it rained after 18 august after successful completion of dam.

In fact i inspected the dam in the night 7.30 pm coming back from Delhi via Nagpur and was worried about the dam. My Range officer Mr. D.S. Dondway told me that pitching and everything is completes now no problem with rains. I just said that now God can rain and vows down for help of God.

Range officer Mr. Dondway was a sincere and intelligent range officer who took all courage to complete the dam in Time.

It is important to mention the cooperation of Then Collector of the District Seoni Mr. V S Niranjan and Superintendent of Police Mr. R.K. Gupta and their families which came to the site in the ceremony to inaugurate the opening of work of the Alikatta dam Help of District administration is very crucial and important for the success of your project and specially new destination of wild tourism.

Water and grasses near water body helped to increase tiger population and I am told that one tigress of Pench has given 4 -5 cubs and all survived.

It is recorded that legendry tigress Collarwali which gave 26 cubs in a span of 13 yrs from 2004–05 born till 2017–18, and if you count cubs given by her progeny together that will count to 50 odd number.

This is the beauty of proper conservation, sufficient water throughout park and habitat management that one tigress can contribute 50 tigers in a span of 13 years. Tigers are prolific breeders and to protect them you have to have sufficient water, sufficient prey base and protection against poaching.

Construction of Dykes for retaining water:-
Dyke is a structure that like small dam which is constructed in the neck of a small nala joining the Pench river. Here due to Totaladoh dam large area of park (60sqkm) comes under

submergence and after water is receded riverbanks becomes marshy land and wild animals cannot go to drink water in the river hence if we stop the nala (stream) in neck of river we can impound large quantity of water in a saucer shape area or a tank with very low cost. I have discussed it in previous Chapter as to how dykes have been constructed in Pench Tiger Reserve area. I have constructed 3 dykes at three different points namely:

1. Alikatta dyke number one
2. Alikatta dyke number two
3. Purethadi.

These dykes became the breeding and hunting places for tigresses. Due to water and green Doob grasses (Cynodon dactylon), large number of spotted deer(Axis axis) and Sambar(Cervus unicolor) concentrate in this area resulting in abundant prey which is ideal for breeding place of tigress. Though there is no rocks and small caves to hide the small cubs but thick lantana bushes present in the area used for shelter of small tiger cubs.

I had constructed about 25 small dams and it was found that all these water bodies were found to be breeding places for tigress.

(2) Disturbance and Habitat loss of National Park Due to Kumbha Baba Mela and Nag Mela:-

Kumbha Baba mela use to happen in the month of January inside park for a week in which tribal of 100 odd villages gathered thousands in number and stay there inside Park and they perform Drama in stage with very loud speakers throughout night. They go to a hillock khairvanmatta in the top of that hill there is a tree where they worship Kumbha Baba a saint of olden time. There is a hollow place in tree root where grains are donated and it is said that any tribal in need can take grains and should return equal amount after some time. But this was Destroying the core tiger habitat.

After study the problem in the year 2002 I made an effort to change the venue of Mela outside Park in the ground of Karmajhiri after persuading tribal and other local leaders, could succeed with great difficulty and this was a great step forward for conservation of park. Similarly a big mela was to organize in Chhindwara side of Park in the name of Nag Mela where people come to worship Nag (Snake God) which was in core area, which was stopped by me with great persuasion to people and being firm.

(3) Man animal conflict and win - win solution:-

Pench tiger Reserve Seoni has no village inside National park and sanctuary that is a plus point but there are 100 odd villages adjoining park area within 5 km radius to the boundary of park, some of the villages are very big with 300–500 house hold and lot of cattle population which are potential pressure to park habitat and habitat of buffer and a potential conflict zone on amount of cattle kill, human kill by wild animals, grazing by domestic cattle inside park as well as crop raiding by herbivores from the agriculture fields of farmers adjoining park area.

(i). Construction of Cattle proof wall along the boundary of National Park and Sanctuary:-

Chhindwara side of park area was very vulnerable to cattle grazing inside park area and other unlawful activity including illegal fishing in Totaladoh dam and even poaching of wild animals.

So to avoid crop raiding by our wild animals and also to stop grazing of grass inside park area by domestic cattle we planned to construct cattle proof wall made of random rubble stones of the size 2mtx1mt x 1.8mt i.e 2meter base x1.8 meter height x 1 meter top width.

This was so effective and natural that wild animals did not go to villager's field so it helped to save their agricultural crop and it has helped to solve problem of crop raiding which was a regular problem and measure conflict between park authorities and villagers.

This cattle proof wall helped to save our grass and habitat in Chhindwara side of park and it is said that this area was almost devoid of spotted deer in earlier time now is full of spotted deer Bison, and Sambar etc. due to improved habitat.

(ii) Cattle kill and anger of people a measure conflict:-
Cattle kill by tiger is a measure conflict between people and wild animals and this was a cause of concern to avoid poisoning of tiger and panther by pouring Aldrine in cattle kill to poison tiger.

This can only be stopped if we pay compensation promptly with in fortnight without any cumbersome procedure to owner of the cattle. A case has to be prepared by forester taking tracing of pugmarks of tiger or may be plaster cast and Veterinary doctor has to certify the carnivore animal who killed cattle and this procedure takes very long time and owner has to run to bring veterinary doctor and forest staff to the place of kill this cast too much to poor owner of cattle and he gets compensation very late and net gain is very less as he has to spend money to follow procedure.

This is the main cause of poisoning of tiger due to cattle kill.

I had made a system where cattle herdsman will inform the nearby staff about the kill and he will get 500 rupees for giving information under "Van Surksha Purskar Niyam" if he informs the incidence same day without disturbing tiger to eat the cattle, if he reports next day he will get 300 rupees and for further delay he will not get any reward but he may be barred to graze his cattle in that forest area.

Forest staff have to make list of cattle herders grazing their herd in different forest area in buffer and adjoining forest area so that they can communicate with them and they can be made informers to tell about the tiger movement and also about any illegal immigrant or outsider poachers so that we can prevent poaching.

After getting information from herders forest guard will inform higher officers and concern forester and range officer will see that compensation case is timely cleared and owner of the cattle gets full compensation with in fort night. This scheme was very successful and we could save a tigress operating in jamtara -Gumtara side with 4 cubs and killing two cattle daily. This scheme should be implemented by all P A managers to save the tigers and avoid man animal conflict.

(iii) Fishing in Totaladoh Dam inside National park:

Totaladoh Dam area inside Pench tiger Reserve Seoni (M.P) is approx. 60 Sq km and in Pench Tiger reserve Maharashtra 20 sq km.

Large number of fish found in dam but due to wildlife protection act nobody can fish inside park but surrounding villagers do lot of illegal fishing inside park area in Dam both side of M.P. and Maharashtra which threatens the tiger and herbivore population. There is lot of disturbance in night and also danger of poaching.

So we along with Maharashtra forest Deptt., Successfully coordinated to catch approximately 200 boats which were used in catching fish. For this we employed local youth and they gave information as where they put the boats inside deep water and we seized all of them. With regular patrolling we stopped fishing in dam to a great extent but small amount of fishing may not be ruled out.

This was a great achievement and the then S.D.O. forest Chhindwara area was awarded with "Amrita devi Vriksh Mitra purskar" a citation and 50000 rupees for his work on protection to wild life and controlling fishing in Totaladoh on my recommendation.

(4) Eco Development of Villages and winning Public Support:

Eco development project under JEF project of World Bank aims at overall development of villages surrounding PA area to reduce pressure on park. Number of developmental works was undertaken which includes:

- (i.) Development of agriculture Fields (Constructing earthen mounds around fields)
- (ii.) Construction of Small tanks in village area for irrigation and water for day to day utilization, drinking water for cattle.
- (iii.) Construction of Wells and Hand pumps for drinking water
- (iv.) Construction of biogas plants to save forest by replacing fuel wood by biogas for cooking of food.
- (v.) Employment generating Works

Other Initiative:

Preventive and cure of Malaria fever:

Malaria Fever among Local Villagers:

Malaria fever is rampant in surrounding villages in both districts and poor families spending 3000–5000 rupees annually normally on treatment of malaria fever but sometimes it goes very high if case becomes serious. To prevent malaria fever i have successfully introduced an herbal preparation which prevents as well as it cures malaria fever.

Kalmegh (*Andrographis penniculata*) a small plants is found in the forest is used for this. Panchang of Kalmegh dried plant 50 gram is boiled in one liter of water till one fourth is remaining then it is cooled.

20 ml Quath early in the morning by an adult for a month or at least 15 days prevents malaria and other fevers. For cure one has to take this amount morning and evening for 15 days and half of this should be taken by children.

We have distributed packets of kalmegh Panchang to each families through eco development committee with their developmental fund created by eco development project. This was so successful that villagers had faith with wild life Deptt., and they started cooperating in conservation initiative.

Malaria Fever among Field Staff:
Our Field staff and subordinates were also suffering from malaria and 30% of staff used to go on leave or absent or ill so the use of Kalmegh help to make all staff healthy and working. This is very important management principle to keep your working force healthy and fit also to save their money so that they are not poor and they save money from treatment.

Grain Bank For Poor Villagers:
It has come to my notice that our 60% population are agriculture laborers and they work in the farms of rich farmers. Laborers have marginal farm land and mostly dependent upon doing wages in others farms for which they are given advance money in summer to work for whole year in the farms with almost half the prevailing wage rate because they took advance in summer. This was plight of poor farmers so I planned grain bank scheme in

which as per requirement of village poor population we will give one quintal rice to each family free of cast from Development fund available in the eco committee to be returned in next season with extra 10% either in cash or in kind i.e. Rice.

This rice returned from each farmer will be distributed to same farmers in next summer so that they do not become bonded labor and with this they got full wages which was double to the wages given when they were given advanced money.

At that time wages they got was 40 rupees when paid full and bonded labor got only 20 rupees. This scheme helped to enhance the income of poor farmers which were 60% of the population. This helped to generate Goodwill among villagers.

Preventing Forest fires in P A:

Forest fires are mostly man made and it is caused by local villagers due to anguish with staff or to collect certain forest produce. Pench Tiger Reserve used to have forest fires very frequently and large areas were used to burn.

But we explained to villagers that if you lit fire in forest then slowly Kalmegh plants will disappear and your future generation will be deprived of kalmegh for treating and preventing Malaria.

This along with other initiative was helpful to protect forest from fire.

Human Resource Management:

This is the most important issue to be tackled in order to take your Park to new height in respect of protection, tourism promotion and responsive administration.

When I was posted Pench tiger reserve was not in the list of tourist destination so staff posted was not feeling as if they are important if they compared it to adjoining Kanha Tiger Reserve or Bandhavgarh Tiger reserve.

Kanha and Bandhavgarh were very famous tiger reserve and due to VIP tourists staff feel elevated so is the case with tiger reserve that is given more funds and treated differently.

My job was to elevate the moral of staff and take Pench Tiger reserve to new heights in field of tourist influx and better conservation, which I did.

Pench Tiger reserve became number one tiger reserve in the year 2010. In the year 2006 it came above Bandhavgarh and in subsequent evaluation in the year 2010 it topped the list in India and became number one in India.

Number of measure was taken to keep staff in good mood by giving their dues in time and without trouble.

Field staff was suffering from malaria time and again and almost 30% staff was ill or absent from duty due to illness and spending lot of money on health, this has been tackled by innovation of Kalmegh plant for preventing malaria fever and its cure. This has proved to be in favour of management.

Reward: One Forest Guard Mr. Gautam Soni was given out of turn promotion for his excellent work in constructing jhiriya in a hillock for drinking water to wild animals.

Mr. Ravikant Mishra S.D.O. Chhindwara area of Pench Tiger reserve was awarded with Amritadevi Vishnoi Reward for his excellent work in controlling fishing in Totaladoh Dam inside PA.

Some Interesting event and experiences:
1. Female elephant Chanchala kumari illness and cure by Herbal Medicine:
A female Elephant named as Chanchala kumari whose age was about 55–60 yrs and was in the park since a decade but it became pregnant for the first time and its male calf died inside

which was taken out with difficulty. Mahavats could not tell the correct time of mating and gestation period is 24 months so calf died in ovary but due to this she use to discharge white water in liters and was seriously ill due to white discharge. We consulted from Kerala and Karnataka and searched for medicine by our Veterinary Doctor Mr. Akhilesh Mishra And Mr. A.B. Shrivastav of Veterinary college but found no drug but reference of death of an elephant was there. We send it to Veterinary college Jabalpur for a month but her health was deteriorating day by day then i ordered to bring back elephant to forest in natural surroundings.

Then i asked an old forest guard as to what Ayurvedic medicine we give in case of White discharge in Women, he told me they give palashbel climber(Butea superva) with gud (jaggery) so i thought that it can work if given in more quantity. So we started giving palashbel climber about one feet length and 250 gram jaggery daily. Elephant was all right in 15 days and she herself used to go in forest and eat Palashbel on own.

So this way we saved one elephant from white discharge illness for which there was not any cure known to any vet doctor.

2. Tigress Death and Rearing of her two Cubs in forest:
It was April month in the year 2003 when a tigress of Pawarjhiriya was seen with wound in her back and doctor advised me to do surgery on her to save her and her 2 cubs one male and another female of 5 month old and if not operated soon we will lose all three.

I talked to Chief Wild Life Warden and Director project tiger for giving permission to operate tigress as tiger is schedule one. I got positive reference from both and Director Project

Tiger Delhi Mr. Rajesh Gopal Told me to send request letter from CWLW and he will immediately give permission by fax.

I called team of Doctors to operate Tigress but on that day CWLW Mr. A.P. Dwivedi declined to give permission on the ground that it is not Zoo let it die.

And Tigress died within fortnight and cubs were orphaned. I placed on Forest Guard Mr. Vijay Patel with one elephant and told not to touch them, they were in cave and were safe with water in Pawarjhiriya tank which they were seen using which was just nearby within half a kilometer. We started serving mutton at cave sitting in elephant and observed that they were eating properly. This continued for Six month when our guard found that they killed on small chital infant and were seen eating.

These cubs were found eating with another tigress named as Kankati of Kalaphad with her two cubs. It is first time that we could see the tigress which was sister of their mother tigress was helping these cubs in feeding. These cubs might have gone accidently to the kill made by that tigress and waited to eat after her cubs and tigress did allow. So now we were relieved from the care of cubs but watching their movements. Male cub became the strong Tiger popularly known as charger and commanded big area and dominated for a decade.

This is the only story of rearing 5 moth old tiger cubs in nature without touching them. we would have reared them even if another tigress could not allowed them to share her kill by supplying them feed till they were 2 yrs old. So this was an interesting story that people must know that tiger cubs can be reared in nature without touching them, otherwise their fate would have been to be sent to zoo and whole of their life would have been in captivity.

Success:

Pench Tiger reserve became number one tiger reserve in the year 2010. In the year 2006 it came above Bandhavgarh and in subsequent evaluation in the year 2010 it topped the list in India and became number one in India. Foreign Tourist influx increased tremendously.

In The year 2014 evaluation year also Pench Tiger Reserve stood first among all tiger reserves in India but NTCA thought out not to disclose the numbering and position of different tiger reserve to avoid exposing some Tiger reserve so they published the data in Grading like A,B,C, etc. Tiger Reserve scored 80% or more will come in first category and so on.

It was a remarkable success for Pench tiger reserve to become number one tiger reserve in India beating most famous Kanha Tiger reserve in a short span of time, because of proper management without tears.

It is one of the best Tiger reserve having highest prey base and high growth of tiger population in India. It is best managed tiger reserve in habitat and water management and also with very little man animal conflict.

One interesting thing which must be shared and that is My Spiritual Guruji Swami Sachidanand Maharaj Dharkundi district Satna visited my park in the year 2003 and written in visitor's book that this National park will be ahead of Bandhavgarh and Kanha in coming years. His Future prediction came true and Pench tiger Reserve became number two beating Bandhavgarh National park in 2006, four year evaluation result published by NTCA, where Kanha was number One in M.P. But in 2010 evaluation Report by NTCA for all tiger reserve in India, Pench Tiger Reserve stood number one tiger reserve in India leaving behind Kanha

Tiger reserve as number Two. This way future prediction by Most Honorable Dharkundi Maharaj came true within same sequence.

I also told Mr. Khageswar Naik my senior IFS who was Field Director Kanha National park at my time that i will make Pench tiger reserve in such a way that it will supersede Kanha Tiger reserve in very short time and see it happened in just 7 yrs in 2010 when Mr. Khageswar Naik himself was posted as Field director Pench tiger reserve. He also praised work done by me specially water management and Cattle proof wall in Chhindwara side to prevent cattle from grazing inside core area.

So we can say that Practical approach with innovative ideas is the key to success of wild life management in an area and this is what is called wild life management without tears.

Sir William Henry Sleeman
(1788 – 1856)

नरभेड़िया : लेफ्टिनेंट जॉन मूर द्वारा बनाये गये स्केच की विष्णु अग्निहोत्री निर्मित अनुकृति

Joseph Rudyard Kipling

Kalmegh (*Andrographis Penniculata*)

Hand pump: Photo by R. G. Soni

Saucer: Photo by R. G. Soni

Jhiriya: Photo by R. G. Soni

Jhiriya: Photo by R. G. Soni

Nala Bandhan: Photo by R. G. Soni

Spotted Deer herds around Dyke: Photo by R. G. Soni

Alikatta Tank: Photo by R. G. Soni

Dyke in right Hand full of Water (River bed dry in left hand): Photo by R. G. Soni

Barheded Goose in Dyke: Photo by R. G. Soni

Water Storage in Dyke I Alikatta: Photo by R. G. Soni

Bar headed goose: Photo by R. G. Soni

Mowgli Hut: Photo by R. G. Soni

Tank: Photo by R. G. Soni

Tank: Photo by R. G. Soni

Mowgli Huts: Photo by R. G. Soni

Raiya Kassa Watch tower: Photo by Pradeepti Soni

Malabar pied Hornbill: Photo by R. G. Soni

Submergence area: Photo by Pradeepti Soni

Safari Ride Alikatta: Photo by Pranay Soni

Tiger sighting from elephant back: Photo by Pranay Soni

Tiger Sighting: Photo by Pranay Soni

Mowgli Hut (Year 2002): Photo by Pranay Soni

Bison Herd: Photo by Pradeepti Soni

Spotted Deer herds in Submergence Area Pench Tiger Reserve: Photo by R.G. Soni

Kullu Tree (Sterculia urens) Ghost Tree: Photo by R.G. Soni

Brahminy Ducks: Photo by R. G. Soni

Indian Bison: Photo by R. G. Soni

Sambar Stag: Photo by Jagdish chandra

Wild Dogs on kill

Tiger: Photo by Jagdish chandra

Dense Forest Pench Tiger Reserve: Photo by R.G.Soni

Tiger: Photo by R. G. Soni

**Typical Feature of Pench Tiger Reserve
(Ficus species over Rock):** Photo by Jagdish chandra

Grey Wolf: Photo from Pench Office

Tiger: Photo by Jagdish Chandra

Tiger: Photo by Jagdish chandra

Herds of Spotted Deer: Photo by R.G.Soni

Wild Dog on hunting: Photo by Jgdish Chandra

Alikatta Ground: Photo by Jgdish Chandra

Kumbha Baba Mela in Karmajhiri Village

Kumbha Baba Mela

Pilgrims to Kumbha Baba Hillock

Akshya Bhandar Cave Kumbha Baba Place in Khairvanmatta Hillock

Lesser Adjutatant Stork: Photo by R. G. Soni

Dense Forest in Pench Tiger Reserve: Photo by R. G. Soni

Spotted Deer stag: Photo by Pranay Soni

Peacock: Photo by Pranay Soni

BIBLIOGRAPHY

Ranjitsingh M.K. 2017 "A Life with wild life", Harper Collins Publishers India.

Strandel R.A. "Seonee, Camp life in Satpuda Hills".

Surgent and Carter, 1999 Wild Life Management.

Strandel R.A. "Seonee, Camp life in Satpuda Hills " for process of construction of tank.

Shaw, 1985 describing cover for wild life.

Prater S.H., C.M.Z.S. The Book of Indian Animals.

Pabla H.S. 2015, Wild life conservation in India -1, Road to Nowhere.

ABOUT THE AUTHOR

Dr. Ram Gopal Soni IFS is from Indian forest Service (1982) Batch has worked in various capacities in Madhya Pradesh Forest Deptt. starting from Divisional forest officer in various Divisions, conservator of Forest, Field  Director Pench Tiger Reserve Seoni, Chief Conservator of Forest Balaghat, Jabalpur and Retired as Additional Principal Chief Conservator Of Forest and Member secretary State Biodiversity Board in the year 2014.

He is credited with Discovery of The Jungle Book Area and the True story Of Mowgli in Pench Tiger Reserve area. He has written three books on Biodiversity one book on Forest Mensuration. He is Ph. D in Tribal Economy and Non Wood Forest Produce, LL.B., M.A. Economics, M.sc. Forestry, AIFC Diploma, M.B.A. (HRD).

He is a keen observer of Nature and wild life and he is credited to make Pench tiger Reserve an unknown wild life area to rise to number one Tiger reserve in the country and his innovative ideas made Pench Tiger Reserve as best water managed area to highest prey base area per square kilometer.